Revitalizing Interculturality in Education

China is often seen as a monolith outside its borders. However, heterogeneity and interculturality have characterized the Middle Kingdom for centuries. Today, China's take on diversity is too easily disparaged or perceived as ambiguous – as if China is not able to take part in impartial conversations about diversity.

The authors wish to contribute to global discussions about interculturality in education, which have often been dominated by 'Western' voices, by problematizing a very specific Chinese perspective called Minzu ('ethnic') education. Minzu is presented as a potential companion to other forms of diversity education (multicultural, intercultural, transcultural, cross-cultural and global education). Without claiming that they have found a miraculous and one-size-fits all recipe, they argue that the lessons learned from researching various aspects of Minzu in Chinese education can also help students, researchers, educators, and decision-makers unthink and rethink the central issue of interculturality. As such the book introduces the complexity, contradictions and benefits of Minzu while helping the reader consider how compatible and complementary it could be with discussions of interculturality in other parts of the world. The book also aims at making readers observe critically their own contexts.

This book was written with an open mind and it should be read with the same.

Fred Dervin is Professor of multicultural education at the University of Helsinki, Finland. He specializes in intercultural education, the sociology of multiculturalism, and student and academic mobility.

Mei Yuan is Associate Professor at the School of Education, Minzu University of China. She specializes in Minzu and intercultural education.

Dervin and Yuan's work, *Revitalizing Interculturality in Education*, comes just in time! The COVID crisis has laid bare the need to fundamentally alter how we think about 'the other,' and indeed who 'the other' is. Dervin and Yuan's work helps us to un-think and re-think what intercultural means in these historic times. Through a detailed discussion of Chinese Minzu education, they suggest the West has much to learn from the Chinese ways of discoursing about interculturality as represented by Minzu education. At a time when scholars in every academic field are rethinking some of their core assumptions, this work has the potential to turn the field of intercultural education on its head. Bravo!

Etta Kralovec, *Professor, University of Arizona, USA*

This book provides a fusion of perspectives from scholars of diverse cultures that enriches the discussion of intercultural education. This latest work by Dervin and Yuan is unique in utilising the focus of Minzu education which provides a flexible approach, that is simultaneously both complex and harmonious, as a perspective for informing and progressing knowledge and practice for intercultural education globally.

Karen Trimmer, *Professor, School of Education,*
University of Southern Queensland, Australia

I congratulate Dervin and Yuan on this valuable contribution to international discussions on intercultural education. With ferocious conviction, they have managed to shed significant new light on the need to find new 'companions' like Minzu education in rethinking interculturality. The reader will emerge changed by it and with a broad understanding of this complex Chinese perspective.

Fengqiao Yan, *Professor, School of Education,*
Peking University, China

To my knowledge no book has taken on Chinese contributions to interculturality in education so seriously and successfully. Adopting a balanced view of the subject matter, the authors manage to challenge, deconstruct and reconstruct a global field of research that will matter even more immensely post-COVID 19. *Revitalising Interculturality* represents a new milestone in Dervin and Yuan's already very impressive work.

Liangang Tian, *General Director, Department of Education*
and Technology, State Ethnic Affairs Commission

Revitalizing Interculturality in Education

Chinese Minzu as a Companion

Fred Dervin and Mei Yuan

Routledge
Taylor & Francis Group

LONDON AND NEW YORK

First published 2022
by Routledge
2 Park Square, Milton Park, Abingdon, Oxon OX14 4RN

and by Routledge
605 Third Avenue, New York, NY 10158

Routledge is an imprint of the Taylor & Francis Group, an informa business

British Library Cataloguing-in-Publication Data
A catalogue record for this book is available from the British Library

Library of Congress Cataloging-in-Publication Data
Names: Dervin, Fred, 1974- author. | Yuan, Mei, 1986- author.
Title: Revitalizing interculturality in education : Chinese minzu as a
    companion / Fred Dervin, Mei Yuan.
Description: Abingdon, Oxon ; New York, NY : Routledge, 2022. |
    Includes bibliographical references and index.
Identifiers: LCCN 2021013043 (print) | LCCN 2021013044 (ebook) |
    ISBN 9781138486867 (hardback) | ISBN 9781351044554 (ebook)
Subjects: LCSH: Multicultural education—China.
Classification: LCC LC1099.5.C6 D47 2022 (print) | LCC LC1099.5.C6
    (ebook) | DDC 370.1170951—dc23
LC record available at https://lccn.loc.gov/2021013043
LC ebook record available at https://lccn.loc.gov/2021013044

ISBN: 978-1-138-48686-7 (hbk)
ISBN: 978-1-032-07412-2 (pbk)
ISBN: 978-1-351-04455-4 (ebk)

DOI: 10.4324/9781351044554

Typeset in Bembo
by Apex CoVantage, LLC

Contents

Figures

Tables

Foreword

In 1759 Samuel Johnson published *The History of Rasselas, Prince of Abissinia*. A gentle satire like Voltaire's *Zadig*, the novel is about a Prince's escape from his dull Abissinian kingdom (Happy Valley) in order to find a 'happy' place on earth. After much disappointment, unable to find happiness, he travels back to Happy Valley. In chapter XI of this Bildungsroman, the Prince's poet-friend, Imlac, describes the world as he has experienced it, praising the Europeans with whom he had conversed. The Prince inquires about them:

> 'By what means,' said the Prince, 'are the Europeans thus powerful? or why, since they can so easily visit Asia and Africa for trade or conquest, cannot the Asiatics and Africans invade their coast, plant colonies in their ports, and give laws to their natural princes? The same wind that carries them back would bring us thither.'
>
> 'They are more powerful, sir, than we,' answered Imlac, 'because they are wiser; knowledge will always predominate over ignorance, as man governs the other animals. But why their knowledge is more than ours I know not what reason can be given but the unsearchable will of the Supreme Being.'

There is no Happy Valley for interculturality in education – the topic of this book. The whole world has to deal with this thorny and complex issue. Different ways of 'doing', theorizing and preparing for interculturality are available around the world. Some perspectives are better known than others. Some perspectives are 'sold' as being better than others – leaving behind other perspectives that could be considered to 'heal' some of the ills that damage interculturality such as social injustice, inequality, discrimination and xenophobia. Yet they all share something in common: *when it comes to diversity, there is no magic formula*. I believe that we all have something to bring to the table. I believe that we can and should all enter into meaningful dialogues around interculturality in education.

Through my long career as a specialist of Minzu 'minority' education in China, I have had the opportunity to meet up with specialists of diversity education from around the world. Although my work has been quite influential in China, I have always found it hard to get our voice heard about interculturality in the 'Western' world and share our own research and educational experiences. I have always been treated with respect and hospitality during my trips abroad for conferences and seminars. Yet I have felt that my voice as a Chinese specialist of issues that concern the entire world was not always treated with 'genuine' generosity. My experience has often been that of 'floating past each other': my American and European counterparts talk about 'their' multicultural and/or intercultural education theories, methods and practices in certain ways and I spoke about 'my' ways – the links between us never really being made. In these 'floating' moments, however, I have noticed on many occasions that we share very similar problems and opportunities.

More importantly, Imlac's ironic words about 'Europeans being powerful' in Johnson's *Rasselas* somewhat resonate with me. Although many Western scholars have shown an interest in Minzu education and in my work, at the end of the day, we end up with Western knowledge systematically winning over. Take as a proof the lack of publications about interculturality in education referring to Chinese Minzu education in international journals. Don't get me wrong, there are publications about Minzu education available in English, however, I believe that they do not always do justice to the opportunities and achievements that it represents.

For the past three years Fred Dervin, Mei Yuan and myself have dedicated our time to researching various aspects of interculturality through the complex lens of Minzu education. China represents a rich and rewarding context of research on diversity education, of which very few Western scholars are aware. This context has its own specificities while, we have argued, it shares similarities with other contexts in terms of interculturality. The theories, concepts/notions, methods and practices that have been developed in the field for the past 40 years deserve to be presented to global audiences, discussed, tested and augmented through international dialogues.

Dervin and Yuan have managed to produce a book which tells the reader why Minzu education matters to the world, what it can bring to those working on interculturality in education and allow them to reflect on their own perceptions and ideologies, but also practices. I am delighted that, thanks to this long overdue book, Minzu education is entering the global 'realm' of intercultural education.

Professor Sude, Minzu University of China
Beijing, 10 February 2021

Introduction

In his ceiling painting entitled *Divine Wisdom Giving the Laws to the Kings and Legislators* (1827), which was made especially for the French State Council rooms at the Louvre, French artist Jean-Baptiste Mauzaisse (1784–1844) depicted the Prophet Moses, Louis XVIII and other kings, as well as 'diverse' legislators receiving the Law from Divine Wisdom, Prudence, Equity and Clemency. Among the legislators one can identify: the first king of Rome Romulus, the first president of the United States George Washington, and the lawgiver of Sparta Lycurgus. In the lower right corner of this 'multicultural patchwork' sits the only Asian figure of the painting: the Chinese philosopher Confucius (551–479 BC). Although China was (still) popular in Europe in the 19th century, figures like Confucius were rarely represented in European art, especially in such an important piece looking over the activities of the State Council. The lack of consideration for anything related to Chinese thought has been somewhat of a constant in Europe and many other parts of the world, even today.

Examining and adding to the polysemic notion of interculturality, this book contributes to discussions of interculturality by proposing to revitalize it through the Chinese notion of Minzu (民族). The verb *to vitalize*, *to give life to*, appeared in the English language around the 1670s and in its figurative sense by 1805. Our goal is to 'give life to' new visions of interculturality, expanding on the scholarship from the past 70 years, when the field of intercultural communication appeared, and including a voice which has been systematically excluded from such discussions by both Western and Chinese scholars. This book is thus a direct reaction to the lack of diversity in the field of Intercultural Communication Education (ICE). This broad field, where interculturality is taught and researched, is interdisciplinary and concerns, for example, business studies, health care, language studies, and teacher education. At first sight, the 'intercultural' appears to be a mish-mash of a concept, used by policymakers, businessmen, educators and scholars.

DOI: 10.4324/9781351044554-1

Current critiques of the field note that theories, methods and practices tend to be overly Euro-/Western-centric[1] and reproduce unequal knowledge power relations. Although ICE is meant to help people think 'otherwise', try to open up to other ways of reflecting and being, and question the current knowledge and practices, based on overtly dominating ideologies, what the field does is to impose ways of thinking about interculturality that tend to ignore the diverse ways of thinking about and 'doing' it around the world. As such, a study by Peng et al. (2020) notes that the most quoted scholars in the field are US- or UK-based, white and English speakers. For a field that strives to discuss and address the position of diverse individuals in education and beyond, this limits the spheres of intellectual engagement with, for example, issues of equality-equity, social justice and encounters beyond borders. Looking at the list of dominating voices identified by Peng et al. (2020), one cannot help noticing that these Western scholars use similar concepts and notions in English, without questioning systematically their potential geopolitical and multilingual meanings or their 'social lives' (e.g. culture, community, respect, tolerance, etc.); emphasize cultural difference over similarity; (somewhat naively) urge people to avoid conflicts and misunderstandings; see diversity negotiations as something linear rather than complex and unstable; and, finally, avoid discussing economic, socio-political and ethical elements openly when dealing with interculturality (see Dervin, 2016). Their emphasis on 'culture' represents what we call Western 'old-fashioned-ism', relying on modern ideologies from the 18th century that have been imposed on the rest of the world (see Maffesoli, 1997). Finally, we note that many of these dominating voices, whose importance and contribution we are obviously not denying here, also cooperate with either the business world (see Hofstede insights: www.hofstede-insights.com; Bennett's IDR Institute: www.idrinstitute.org) and/or supranational organizations (the Organization for Economic Co-operation and Development (OECD) (Paris) www.oecd.org; the Council of Europe www.coe.org), whose ideologies are imposed upon educators around the world, without paying much attention to local contexts. Most 'users' of these models are unaware of the 'groundwater' of these ideologies, and of the potential contradictions that they represent in contrast to people's beliefs and (glocalized) ideologies. It is true that some scholars and educators have been critical of certain 'Western' concepts and theories that contribute to 'box us in' (culture, identity, community, race . . .) and attempted to invert or reject them (e.g. Holliday, 2010). We should be grateful for this questioning since it allows us to discuss and consider anew interculturality. However, we argue that these concepts and theories appear to remain at the foundation of most discussions of interculturality and prevent us from considering other ways of thinking about the notion.

Although we are dissatisfied with the way interculturality is dealt with in its current Western-centric format, in this book, we prefer to use the notion over other terms which have now saturated the market: *multicultural, polycultural, transcultural, cross-cultural*, but also *global* and *postcolonial*. Like interculturality, all these terms are polysemic and connoted somewhat differently in many and varied contexts and by their 'users'. However, in the very word *interculturality*, we are attracted by the aspects of *inter-* and *-ality* of the notion, although we remain unsatisfied with the polysemic and sometimes empty idea of *culture*. *Inter-* and *-ality* stimulate us to think about engagement with diversity in education from dynamic, dialogical and interactive perspectives. As a reminder, the very word *dialogue* in English finds its origin in a Greek word, whose root, *DIA*, indicates movement and shifting back and forth. Interestingly, the very word *culture* (文化) in Chinese used to refer to these phenomena: *change, modification* through interaction, but lost these connotations when Western significations of the concept were borrowed. Fang (2019: 9) notes that 文 and 化 used to refer to 'a situation wherein a change takes place for one side or both sides concerned, as a result of their contact with each other' (Fang, 2019: 9). 化 shows a man straight up and one man upside down.

Central arguments

> The crowds who acclaim false prophets bear witness to the intensity of the aspirations mounting to an empty heaven.
>
> (Raymond Aron, 2002: 55)

Interculturality in education tends to revolve around a limited set of global scholars, whose voices dominate research and practices. This domination is unavoidable and we do not claim that it could be otherwise. Our interest in this book is threefold: 1 To warn other scholars and educators about the dominance of these central voices emerging from the 'West'; 2 To make them aware of the problems and consequences of maintaining the *status quo* by letting these voices speak for and over the whole world – even when they pretend to 'regionalize' their perspective by presenting, for example, a 'European' perspective (e.g. Byram, 2020) – and to avoid jumping into patterns laid out by fashionable perspectives; 3 To help them identify companions, complements and potential alternatives to such voices as a mirror to the way they (are made to) conceptualize interculturality. In the title of this book we use the word *companion* and propose Chinese Minzu as a companion to deal with interculturality in education. Etymologically the word *companion* comes from Late Latin *companionem* which means 'bread fellow' (*com*: with, together + *panis*: bread – with whom one eats bread – see also the Spanish 'companero', the Italian 'compagno' and the French 'copain'). The word *companion* thus indicates *sitting at the same table and sharing food, working with each other, treating each other* equally. Interestingly the Chinese word rendered as 'companion' is 朋 (peng), which in Ancient Chinese meant 'those who shared the same gate'.

The choice of the Chinese example used in this book can be justified in different ways:

- Although China has been intercultural from the outset in terms of languages,[2] cultures and worldviews, it has been rarely or stereotypically used to deal with interculturality in education. In other words, China does not seem to fit necessarily into the Western/global 'cookie cutter' of diversity and interculturality. Homogeneity seems to represent one of the limited aspects of the 'imaginarium' created for China by the 'West'. An imaginarium is 'a playful term used to name places or destinations that engage the imagination, like museums or toy stores' (Swain, 2011: 103). In ICE there have been attempts at taking the Middle Kingdom into account but they have often turned into theoretical and methodological stereotypes. For example, in their book entitled *Communicating Effectively[3] with the Chinese* (1998), Ge Gao and Ting-Toomey review 'specific' aspects of Chinese communication such as *Mianzi* (面子, face-directed communication strategies) and Keqi (客气, polite and mannerly) to help foreigners communicate with the Chinese. Although, at first sight, these might appear different – see 'exotic' - they create a sense of imaginarium. What the authors fail to mention is that, although these phenomena might be explained in a way that makes them 'strange', they do resemble phenomena that most people would experience around the world (see e.g. the work of E. Goffman on the idea of *face*, 1955). Beyond such potentially stereotypical use of 'Chinese characteristics' to inform the foreign Other of how to communicate with the Chinese – but not, for example, to co-learn to live together – there have been a few attempts at trying to use 'Chinese knowledge' about interculturality. In Mainland China, the foreign language textbook *Experiencing Global Intercultural Communication: Preparing for a Community of Shared Future for Mankind and Global Citizenship* (Yuxin et al., 2019), which is used for English majors in higher education, is a rare exception. By attempting to combine 'Western' and 'Eastern' perspectives in the textbook, the authors seem to open new and interesting vistas for ICE in China – and potentially elsewhere. However, in a recent article Simpson et al. (forth.) show that, although there is an attempt at introducing 'Chinese knowledge' for interculturality in this book, Western-centric ideologies dominate and take over the few potential contributions of the Chinese knowledge. We argue that it is time to listen to Chinese alternatives for real. Minzu education, an approach that places interculturality at its centre – although it refers to interculturality from within, amongst Chinese citizens – will serve as an example.

• Be it in media, political and even academic discourses, China is often constructed as a 'bad Other' and systematically criticized and negated. While we were writing this book in the middle of the COVID-19 crisis, end of 2020-early 2021, for example, the only national newspaper in Finland (*Helsingin Sanomat*) systematically included negative, controversial and somewhat ridiculing news about China on a daily basis. We do not recognize the China we have researched in these anecdotal and somewhat controversial pieces of news, which reflect ethnocentrism and might tell us more about how Finland is represented by this newspaper than about the realities of China. In research, many critiques of China are in fact political but they are hidden behind pseudo-scientific slash 'identitarian'[4] arguments ('We Europeans'). Since discourses about China and 'everything Chinese' seem to be consistently on the verge of negativity and the imaginarium, there is a need to propose an alternative construction of today's China, through the example of Minzu. Of course, this does not mean that we will present a rosy picture of China. Like all countries, the Middle Kingdom does have 'good' aspects but also faces challenges.

Although many alternatives to Western interculturality have appeared on the educational market over the past decade, they all seem to share the same problem: they mostly emerged from the 'West' (even those promoted by non-Western scholars), they use concepts and notions that circulate from the 'West' and are imposed onto the rest of the world to talk about diversity. Some of these approaches even claim to be 'better' than others and more 'adapted' to our times, even though they tend to recycle concepts and arguments from another time. What is more, they tend to ignore their own biases and ideologies. Finally, they also often represent an illusion of alternatives since they are embedded in 'Western-'driven politics. Interestingly, in a recent review that we read about a book on interculturality, the authors were attacked for ignoring, for example, the 'paradigm of transculturalism' which was said to be more adapted for the 2020s than 'interculturalism'. The reviewer wrote: 'The [book] also ignores the argument being put forward by writers such as . . . that interculturalism is no longer appropriate for the current world context, and that transculturalism.'

There are many problems in this line of argumentation: 1 Both transculturalism and interculturalism are multifaceted and there is not one way of thinking about and 'applying' them; 2 Rejecting a term for another does not necessarily make the situation better, renaming has never made things better if the conditions and discourses are more or less similar. Considering the situation of the world as we are writing this book (early 2021–COVID-19 era), being transculturalism or interculturalism, the situation shows a complete failure of our world in terms of how we see ourselves/others and how we treat the 'Other'[5] – in and through, for example, the media, research and politics.

In this book we argue that researching and teaching interculturality *otherwise*, by being confronted by other ways of thinking about the notion, are necessary to disrupt scholars' and educators' own identity as 'believers' and even 'followers' of certain intercultural strands.

Why Chinese Minzu?

> Real dialogue isn't about talking to people who believe the same things as you.
>
> (Zygmunt Bauman, 2016: n.p.)

Getting acquainted with Chinese ways of discoursing about interculturality, through Minzu, does not mean suggesting that we should copy and/or implement them in our respective contexts. Of course, there might be ideas that deserve being considered as inspiration but it is up to the reader to decide what to do with them. We see the work that we do on Minzu as a way of allowing ourselves to reflect on how we *see* and *do* interculturality in our respective parts of the world – like looking in a mirror – taking stock of achievements, challenges and potential changes.

As we were writing this introduction, a piece of news trended on Weibo (Chinese social media) explaining that the official name of the 'Chinese Distilled Spirits' in English was changed to 'Chinese Baijiu' by the China Wine Industry Association. Although the comparison might appear awkward, we prefer the notion of Minzu in English compared to that of 'Ethnic groups'.

China is a unitary multi-ethnic state. 'Ethnic' Minzu groups are the product of an ethnic classification project started in China in 1953 and finished in 1990. Different terms have been used in English to refer to these different groups: Minzu, ethnic minorities, minority groups, non-Han peoples, local peoples, nationality, nationality groups. In this book we use the term *Minzu* as it avoids misperceptions and inadequate connotations contained in words like *ethnicity, minority, nationality* in English and other languages. They can be politically marked differently in various parts of the world (see Billeter, 2014 for a discussion on translating Chinese terms into other languages).

Fifty-six Minzu group identities and memberships are officially recognized by the Chinese State today. The Han majority represents about 91.5 per cent of the population while the other 55 Minzu groups represent 8.5 per cent (Zang, 2016: 1). In many cases the latter are often socio-economically, culturally and ethnically different from majority Han Chinese, but not necessarily 'poorer' or 'less educated' as is often wrongly suggested. Minzu status appears on people's identity documents and depends on their parents' own status.

China has been described as consisting of different Minzu groups that interact with each other and have been integrated into the Chinese nation during its history. Different Minzu groups are scattered in different territories of the country, with many concentrated on border regions like Kazakhstan, Korea, Mongolia and Russia. There are also five provincial-level ethnic autonomous regions: Inner Mongolia Autonomous Region, Xinjiang Uyghur Autonomous Region, Guangxi Zhuang Autonomous Region, Ningxia Hui Autonomous Region and Tibet Autonomous Region (Sude et al., 2020).

According to Wang and Du (2018): 'it is necessary to point out that ethnic minorities [Minzu] are not a group of homogenous people. The differences within ethnic minorities should not be ignored as well'. It is also important to note that some Minzu minorities have different first languages on top of Chinese, the common language of Mainland China.

For the past three years, we have cooperated on an attempt to contribute diverse knowledge to ICE by researching the potential contributions of Chinese Minzu education. Minzu education is a broad field of research and practice in China that aims, on the one hand, to educate/train people to navigate between their own Minzu and Chinese common culture and language (Mandarin Chinese), creating a sense of 'national unity' (like most countries in the world, see discussions around *séparatisme/separatism* and *laïcité/secularism* in France in early 2021) and, on the other, a type of intercultural education that allows people of different Minzus to live, study and work together. We also note that there is no unified theoretical underpinning of Minzu education in China, apart from the notion of 'plurality within unicity' (see Sude et al., 2020). These rich perspectives are underexplored in the international literature on ICE.

In this short introduction to Minzu in Mainland China, we see that the notion of Chineseness, although it covers all citizens of the country, is much more complex than one would expect. Minzu individuals tend to experience diversity in terms of (amongst others) language, culture, and sometimes worldview/religion. Their identity thus tends to be situated on a continuum of Chineseness and Minzu. The notion thus represents a stimulating way of revitalizing interculturality.

Working method

The objective of this book is not to give interculturality a(nother) right normative scaffolding. It is based on the principles of criticality and reflexivity, which does not mean being against and/or rejecting, for example, 'Western' perspectives on interculturality. The book simply examines and problematizes the ground, the presuppositions, the potential tensions, the constituents and constitution of Minzu to feed in new discussions about interculturality in education.

This book also aims:

- To justify the need for thinking otherwise about interculturality.
- To introduce various facets of Minzu education to international audiences by giving the voice to different individuals (researchers, students and educators) in order to detail the specificities of Minzus, their interactions and co-learning.
- To help readers understand how the knowledge in the book can help them improve their own reflections, understanding and perspectives on interculturality by considering alternatives.
- To urge intercultural specialists to 'dig' into other knowledge such as Minzu to enrich the way they problematize and deal with interculturality in education.

The book also adds to international literature on ICE by offering concrete views, theories and practices that have not been discussed extensively in world literature before, especially as far as interculturality is concerned. It represents the first extensive book that introduces Minzu education as a companion to ICE. Discussions about the issues of translation and language when dealing with ICE as a global field of research and education are included. At the same time the book proposes to dispel some myths and imaginaries about China as a monolith.

We do realize that the notion of Minzu refers to a local national context and that the idea of interculturality might be 'foreign' to discussions of Minzu. However, we believe that transferring and allowing dialogues to take place between this local context and more global ones could make a solid contribution to current discussions of interculturality, rethinking them in more 'intercultural' ways.

Besides being adjacent to the broad field of diversity education (intercultural/multicultural/ . . . education), our book is also located within comparative and international education. According to Birkeland (2016: 79) the aims of comparative and international education are to 'carry out cultural loans, describe best practices, understand the interrelatedness between education and culture, and develop global solidarity as a world citizen'. We are of the same opinion as Birkeland (ibid.) that there is a need to move beyond *cultural essentialism* and the *all-cultural* when comparing educational approaches (reducing self and other to their cultural essence, which is often limited and stereotypical, see Chen & Dervin, 2019), beyond evaluating educational practice from a *monocultural perspective* (which we could label as *ethnocentric*, or the belief that one's group, one's culture is the best and has all the proper answers to problems) and beyond overlooking the interrelation between *globalization and local practices* (often referred to by the portmanteau word *glocalization*, or the enmeshment of the global and the local, see Hansen, 2019). We do not claim that Chinese Minzu education is better than other 'Western' perspectives on interculturality, or that it stands alone in dealing with and learning about interculturality. Our objective is also to take the current calls for complementarity beyond 'false generosity' (Freire, 1971) by taking the time to listen to people's voices. Through our work, we have interacted with hundreds of different people involved in Minzu education, whose voices are put forward in the book.

Our approach also follows four principles proposed by Li and Dervin (2019), which we try to apply here in a non-normative way, in order to open up dialogues between us and others: 1 *Modesty* from all those involved in comparing and complementing forms of interculturality; 2 *Realism*; 3 *Myth hunting*; 4 *Decentring*.

Dealing with Chinese Minzu education is as politically and ethically sensitive as in other parts of the world. Depending on the context, 'Western' perspectives on interculturality also work with sensitive issues such as *cultural difference*, *identity* and *race*, but also their intersections with gender, social class, and so on. If we take the concept of *race*, for example, in a country like Finland where US multicultural education epistemology dominates, the use of the concept is avoided, which creates tensions and even contradictions in intercultural education discourses and practices considering the centrality of the concept in multicultural education theories (Atabong, 2018).

In no way do we wish to present the reader with undue 'bias' about Minzu. Many studies by both 'Western' and Chinese scholars have been published on Minzu education in English and provide us with some entry points. Two edited books about the policies and practices in the education of 'China's national minorities' by Western scholars based in Hong Kong were published in the early 2010s. Although Postiglione's (2013: 3) volume makes an important point that 'the actual content of schooling reflects the state's view of ethnic inter-group processes' (and the potential gap between policies and practices), the chapters tend to draw on negative evaluation of Minzu education by looking exclusively into 'challenges' and 'disparities'. Although slightly more positive, Leibold and Chen's (2014) edited volume describes the efforts to balance diversity and cohesion in China. Yet, the focus is on problems of minority integration, language barriers and negative attitudes towards minorities in China. These two volumes rely heavily on 'Western' intercultural education concepts and notions but also methodologies to examine the context of Minzu education, which appears problematic to describe the contextual complexities. In this book, we use the multiple voices of students and staff at a Minzu University, where students and staff from the 56 Chinese Minzus study, cooperate and live together. Their voices are, obviously, not meant to generalize those of all Minzu people, all the students and staff from this institution or other Minzu universities in China.

Like every existent policy, practice and epistemology, Chinese Minzu education has 'good' and 'bad' points. However, we see our work as a necessary counterhegemonic platform to disrupt the authority and current cognitive injustice represented by 'Western' perspectives (de Sousa Santos, 2010). By problematizing Chinese Minzu education from a more 'open' perspective, starting from the voices of those who experience it, instead of imposing a 'Western' cosmology, we believe that we can contribute to diversifying epistemologies about interculturality in education.

The book is structured as follows:

Chapter 1 reviews and explores the multifacetedness of the notion of Minzu. The complex, sometimes complementary, sometimes contradictory, voices of Minzu experts from different disciplines are examined.

Chapter 2 builds upon the explorations of the first chapter by detailing the specificities of one important field attached to Minzu issues: *education*. Historical, philosophical and scholarly aspects are taken into account.

The idea of Minzu, especially in education, is unknown to many scholars, educators and the 'man on the street'. However, internationalization of higher education means that Minzu education does interact extensively with the rest of the world by both welcoming and sending international students from and to other countries. Chapter 3 thus asks these questions: 'What do their specific positions in relation to this diverse aspect of Chineseness tell us about Minzu?' 'What insights into interculturality are revealed?'

The final chapters look more specifically into Minzu education as a direct contributor to interculturality. Chapter 4 reviews the ways students of Minzu education construct discourses of interculturality, especially in terms of the competences needed to deal with it. Using the metaphor of the smörgåsbord (a Scandinavian style of buffet mixing hot and cold dishes), Chapter 5 discusses how a given context of Minzu education can support students to identify, explore and problematize the multifacetedness of the notion of interculturality. The conclusion to the book recommends pursuing the exploration of alternative, additional and complementary ways of dealing with interculturality in education.

At the end of each chapter, we have listed questions that can be used by the reader to reflect on what they have read, and especially to link what is described of Minzu to their own contexts of interculturality.

We hope that this book will raise our readers' interests in different perspectives on interculturality in education and give them the inspiration to revitalize it. The world that will emerge from the 2020–2021 pandemic crisis will surely need to rethink the way we see each other and enter into meaningful, inclusive and fair dialogues.

Notes

1 Western-centrism and Euro-centrism refer here to ideologies of interculturality dominating research and education around the world. These ideologies are found in publications, teaching and learning materials (textbooks) and supported by 'selected gurus' mostly from 'English-speaking' countries. They are supported by concepts, notions and ideologemes perceived to be exclusively 'Western' and 'European', and presented im-/explicitly as the only 'Truths' about interculturality. They may be clearly defined or polysemic but their polysemy is rarely problematized. Critiquing them – or attempting to give them new meanings/replacing them with alternatives – is often considered as *interculturally incorrect* (e.g. 'tolerance', 'democratic coexistence', 'inclusion', 'citizenship', 'global competence'). It is important to note that 'Europe' and the 'West' contain many alternative ideologies of interculturality but that not all of them are accepted and/or popular. In other words, scholars and educators from this part of the world may not agree with and/or apply these dominating ideologies in their work.

2 Strolling through the Gugong (故宫, i.e. the 'Forbidden City' in Beijing), one can see old signs in both Chinese and Manchu (an East Asian Tungusic language from Manchuria in Northeast China) above the gates and buildings. On Chinese banknotes 'People's Bank of China' appears in Chinese and in four of China's minority languages: Mongol, Tibetan, Uighur and Zhuang.

3 The adverb 'effectively' is a clear indication of the neoliberal contributions of increasing productivity through such intercultural scholarship.

4 This neologism refers to situations where claims of a 'common' (and thus opposed to others) identity are used to disparage the 'Other', here, the Chinese.

5 In the book, the 'Other' refers to anyone who is perceived (and often imagined) to be exclusively different from the 'Self', especially in relation to nationality, ethnicity, language and religion (amongst others).

1 Making sense of the notion of Minzu

Chinese history has been filled with encounters between different groups of people, which have been referred to and classified in many varied and flexible ways throughout the centuries (Harrell, 2000). One of today's official Minzu 'ethnic' groups, the Hui, who are partly adherents of Islam, was already mentioned by Matteo Ricci, the first European Jesuit to reach Beijing in the 16th century. In fact, the Italian priest reports that 'All these Sects the Chinois call, Hoei [Hui], the Jewes distinguished by their refusing to eate the sinew or leg; the Saracens, Swines flesh; the Christians, by refusing to feed on round-hoofed beasts, Asses, Horses, Mules, which all both Chinois, Saracens and Jewes doe there feed on' (Purchas, 2014: 466). Confusion, mislabelling and hybridity seem to have qualified Chinese Minzus throughout history. The year 1985 marked the official categorization of today's Minzu groups in the Middle Kingdom – a process that started in 1949 (Benton Lee, 2016). Represented by 155 minority areas with five autonomous regions, 30 independent prefectures, 120 counties and 1,356 Minzu townships, Minzu groups vary in size and growth (Sude et al., 2020), accounting for 8.41 per cent of the country's total population (Ma, 2017: 130), and 53 have their own languages. According to the Constitution and Law of the People's Republic of China on the Standard Spoken and Written Chinese Language, all Minzus are entitled to use and develop their own spoken and written languages (2004: Article 4).[1] For instance, in Xinjiang, ten different languages are used in administration, broadcasting and television, education, legislation and publishing (*China Daily*, 30.6.2019).

The notion of Minzu is in fact much more complex than the mere naming of different 'ethnic' groups in China. For Zhao (2014: 31), when we try to express the idea of Minzu in English, 'irrespective of which concept of Minzu we employ or which standpoint we take, we are only exchanging one Western model for another, without ever finding a way of identifying and expressing our own Chinese uniqueness'.

DOI: 10.4324/9781351044554-2

Until 1911, China was ruled by the Manchu Minzu from Northeast China. According to Leibold (2016), it is around that time that the notion of Minzu appeared, influenced by Japan. As such, a Qing Dynasty scholar, Liang Qichao (梁启超, 1873–1929), is often reported as having translated the Japanese term *minzoku* (みんぞく) into *Minzu* in the late 19th century, making the notion part of the discourse on the Chinese national state-building and of the nation-state. The Chinese word Minzu is composed of *min* (民) for 'folk or common people' and *zu* (族) for 'consanguinity or lineage'. It was the Communist Party of China that officially made the country a multi-Minzu and unified nation. The identification project, which took many decades, officialized Minzu identities and memberships. What is more, Zhang and Chen (2014: 400) explain that the 1950s marked 'the establishment of Autonomous Regions for concentrated ethnic populations, the coexistence of an ethnic language school system and a Mandarin school system as options for ethnic students to choose from, and preferential treatments in minority students' access to college'. All these were meant to promote cultural diversity, reforms and regional economic development as well as bridging between 'majority' Han and other Minzus. Preferential treatment and policy privileges were widely made available for Minzus, in terms of employment, business development and political representation. As far as education is concerned, remedial programs, preferential admissions and boarding schools for Minzu students are common today.

The influence from outside China on the way Minzus have been classified and discussed in the 20th century is noted by Guo (2020: 17), who asserts: 'when foreign words and ideologies such as race, ethnicity, nation, nationalism, civilisation and society were introduced into China, scholars at that time were struggling to understand these terms and how to relate them to the Chinese context'. The fact that translations of the word Minzu in English and other languages are multiform and somewhat confusing seems to derive from this mix of often a-contextualized ideologies that have penetrated the Chinese field of thought about Minzu.

At the end of the 20th century, some Chinese scholars from different fields of research undertook to unthink and rethink Minzu. This is the case of the anthropologist and sociologist Fei Xiaotong (费孝通, 1910–2005), whose theory on Minzu groups in Chinese history is influential. Fei argues that all the 56 Minzus share an overarching identity which is the result of centuries of cohabitation and interaction, regardless of their differences in terms of language and culture. The anthropologist and sociologist used the phrases 'plural unity pattern' and 'unified multiethnic state' (中華民族多元一體, Fei, 1988) to describe Minzu relations: Minzus are plural and diverse, yet they are united by the fact that they form together the Chinese nation. The Chinese nation is thus both culturally pluralistic and politically unified. For Fei, in order to coexist harmoniously, Minzus need to be aware of and accept each other's unique characteristics and joint identity. Many Chinese scholars but also Chinese policymakers have embraced and implemented Fei's theory (Zhang & Chen, 2014).

However, some Chinese scholars have noted recently further problems with the notion of Minzu. As such Zhang Xiaojun (2017) asserts that Minzu can have many different functions in Chinese society, which adds to its polysemy. He argues (ibid.) that different definitions of Minzu seem to include:

- The United Nations' definition ('ethnic groups'),
- The Chinese national definition based on the official categorization following the creation of the Republic of China,
- An academic definition ('cultural groups'),
- People's identity (self-identification or identification by others).

Another aspect of current debates is described by the same scholar (2017) who suggests, following Ma (2017), that the overemphasis on ethnic issues to deal with Minzu issues makes it too broad as it encompasses cultural, social, religious but also economic issues (such as poverty). He thus argues that Minzu should give way to 'culturalizing policies'. This would entail unifying economic, social, political and cultural fields and pluralizing at Minzu group level. Ma (2017) adds that autonomization and preferential policies could lead to the politicization of Minzu groups, isolate them and create failed Minzu integration. Zhang and Chen (2014: 405) summarize this problem as follows: 'in the attempt to pacify minority groups and enhance social solidarity and national unity, the Chinese authorities had engaged in an active process of establishing, essentialising, and staticising cultural differences between groups'.

In 2014 Zhao Xudong emphasized at least two further paradigm crises concerning Minzu: as a scientific perspective, Minzu does not have a common basis for research, which seems to go hand in hand with some sort of confusion of Minzu politics in China. Zhao (ibid.) is also critical of the influence of Western scholarship on Minzu studies, which adds to its misperception, and does not really allow scholars or educators to explore the specific features of Minzu.

Epistemologically, methodologically, societally, politically and individually, the word Minzu can thus mean different things. As a reminder, in English, it is translated as 'ethnic groups', 'minority groups', 'cultural groups', or 'nationalities' (amongst others). In our work we prefer to keep the Chinese term Minzu since the English words tend to connote extra layers of (politico-economic) meanings that do not seem to fit the Chinese context. The use of the Chinese word in English also forces us, in a sense, to modify our worldview about 'groups' and thus to avoid imposing ideologies that do not necessarily fit into this context.

In this chapter we wish to deepen our understanding of Minzu by exploring discourses of Minzu by interdisciplinary specialists from a specific institution: Minzu University of China (MUC) in Beijing, a hyper-diverse and interdisciplinary institution where members of all the Minzu groups live, study and interact together. In order to give more strength to Minzu as a companion, alternative and complement to interculturality in education, in agreement with Qian (2010: 70), 'explorations into multicultural education must be linked with the political, cultural, and regional situations of multinational unity in China's society'. We argue that listening to how these specialists discuss, construct and problematize Minzu can help us add to the meanings and objectives of Minzu education, especially as a potential inspiration for interculturality in education.

Exploring the voice of Minzu experts from different fields

> A thing is not strange in itself; it depends on me to make it strange.
> (Guo Pu, quoted by Strassberg, 2002: 17)

The idea of Minzu is not an easy one. Politically, theoretically, societally and educationally, although there appear to be some foundational aspects (e.g. 'unity and plurality'), current discussions around Minzu as a term to be used in education show some confusion, disagreement and instability. In our previous discussions of Minzu education (esp. in higher education), and especially with colleagues from the 'West', we have sensed some mistrust and even disregard. Currently, media and political discussions around China in the West often include negative comments about the autonomous territory of Xinjiang in the Northwest of the country (with a focus on Uyghur people) and Tibet. Our assumption is that the confusion and complexity around the notion of Minzu, for example in education in China and abroad, does not help the situation. What is more, the use of concepts such as *ethnic groups* and *unification* in English, which are somewhat 'untranslatables' of the Chinese versions, makes the situation worse.

In what follows we examine how interdisciplinary specialists of Minzu discuss the term and what it entails. Interviews with scholars from MUC, which specialize in Minzu issues, were organized in 2020. In total, ten scholars from the following diverse fields were interviewed: anthropology/ethnology and sociology; Minzu area studies; Minzu ethics; Minzu history; Minzu Marxist theory; Chinese Minzu languages; Traditional Chinese and Minzu medicine. Ten different Minzus were represented: Bouyei, Han, Hui, Kyrgyz, Korean, Mongolian, Tibetan, Tu, Yi and Zhuang. Nine male and one female scholars, whose age ranged between 45 and 80 years old, took part in our study. Table 1.1 provides basic information about the participants who were selected on the basis of representability. Following discussions with colleagues at their schools, we were directed towards them as the best scholars in their fields.

Table 1.1 Information concerning the participants

	Gender	Minzu	Position + field of research	Languages spoken
1	Male	Bouyei	• Academy Professor • Chinese Minzu Languages	• Chinese • Bouyei • Gelao
2	Male	Han	• Professor • Minzu ethics	• Chinese
3	Male	Hui	• Professor • Ethnology and Sociology	• Chinese • Uygur
4	Female	Kyrgyz	• Academy Professor • Chinese Minzu Languages	• Chinese • Seven other languages (e.g. Uyghur, Kazakh, Kirgiz, Kyrgyz)
5	Male	Korean	• Professor • Minzu Marxist theory	• Chinese • Korean
6	Male	Mongolian	• Professor • Minzu history (History of Mongolia and Northern Minzus in the Ming and Qing dynasties)	• Chinese • Mongolian
7	Male	Tibetan	• Professor • Bon research and Taoism	• Chinese Tibetan
8	Male	Tu	• Professor • Anthropology and ethnology	• Chinese • Tu
9	Male	Yi	• Associate Professor • Traditional Chinese and Yi medicine	• Chinese • Yi
10	Male	Zhuang	• Professor • Minzu area studies (Zhuang studies)	• Chinese • Zhuang

A few words about the different Minzus that are represented by our participants are necessary here (in alphabetical order of Minzus):

- The Bouyei people live in the South of China and number approx. 2.5 million. The Bouyei language is very close to standard Zhuang, another Minzu language.
- The Han represent the majority Minzu of China (approx. 91 per cent of Mainland China's population). They trace a common ancestry to the Huaxia, tribes along the Yellow River. The Han speak Chinese and various dialects of the language.
- The Hui are composed of Chinese-speaking adherents of Islam in majority and number approx. 20 million. They are concentrated in Northwest China (e.g. Gansu and Xinjiang).
- Chinese Koreans number roughly 2.5 million people and are located in the Northeast of the country.
- The Kyrgyz (number about 210,000) are found mainly in the Kizilsu Kirghiz Autonomous Prefecture in the Xinjiang Autonomous Region. Kirgiz is a Turkic language.
- Mongols number about 5.8 million people. They live mostly in Inner Mongolia and Xinjiang. Mongolian is an official language of Inner Mongolia and is written in the traditional Mongolian script.
- The Tibetans (approx. 5.5 million people) live mostly in the Tibet Autonomous Region and in different neighbouring regions such as Sichuan and Qinghai.
- The Tu people (approx. 300,000 people) live in the northwestern part of China. They speak a Mongolic language called Monguor.
- The Yi people (approx. 9 million people) live mostly in rural and mountainous areas of the southwest of the country. Yi people speak different mutually unintelligible languages, which belong to the Tibetan-Myanmese language group.
- The Zhuang people (approx. 18 million people) live mostly in the Guangxi Autonomous Region in the South. It is one of the largest Minzus. The Zhuang languages, from the Tai family (including Thai and Lao), are mutually unintelligible.

Each interview lasted for about one hour, was done in Chinese and followed the same protocol. The participants seemed eager to share their views about Minzu and spoke extensively about the points we were trying to prod. This is how we introduced our research:

We are a team of Chinese-Finnish scholars who specialize in inter-cultural and Minzu minority education. Our interest is to contribute to a form of education that treats people equally and make them live, work and study together in harmony.

We have researched different aspects of Minzu education, with a view of enriching international discussions around diversity in education and preparing students to live, work and study together in harmony. We strongly believe that Minzu knowledge and epistemologies, esp. in the way they help all Chinese to live in harmony, can help international scholars and educators to think about education for diversity in different ways. China has a long history of 'interminzu' relations, of which the world is unaware and we believe we should discuss and share this history and its potential benefits today.

Ten questions were then asked to the specialists: introducing oneself, theorizing Minzu, linguistic elements of Minzu languages and the potential benefits of Minzu for education.

After translating the interviews into English and negotiating meanings between us, the analysis was done by means of discourse analysis, in its dialogical form (see e.g. Dervin, 2016). Combing through the interviews, using linguistic elements such as represented discourses (i.e. using the voice of other people to support a claim), subjectively marked terms (such as adjectives and verbs, see Johansson & Suomela-Salmi, 2011), we have identified the specific and complex ways the participants describe and problematize Minzu, especially in terms of interminzu relations.

Characterizing Minzu for the outside world

During the interviews, the specialists were all asked to imagine that they had to introduce the idea of Minzu to 'foreigners'. The following questions were asked: 'How would you describe the Minzu you specialize in/ do research on to a foreigner?', 'What is special about it?', 'What would a foreigner need to know about this Minzu to get a sense of its people?' Our motivation for asking these questions was to see how ready these experts felt they were to explain this complex notion to the outside world (see Ma, 2017). While the majority of them provided some answers, others seemed either unable to do so or their answers seemed off-topic. As can be seen in Figure 1.1 the answers are varied and diverse and open up different perspectives on Minzu.

Going back in history, the specialist of Tibetan Minzu uses an intercultural 'historical' perspective to describe his Minzu to foreigners. It is important to note however that this scholar starts by explaining that the foreigners he has met and discussed his Minzu with, have all been knowledgeable about it:

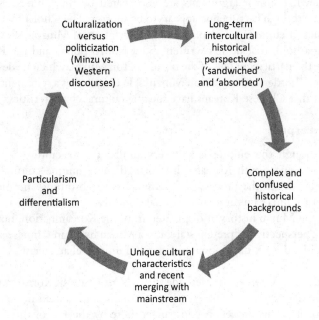

Figure 1.1 Characterizing Minzu for the outside world

Excerpt 1

In some international academic conferences like international university conferences, some international anthropological conferences, international language conferences, and various academic conferences, they are all studying Tibetans. So I haven't fully introduced Tibetans to foreigners.

The main key terms that the scholar uses to describe the Minzu in the rest of his turn are 'sandwiched' and 'absorbed'/'embedded': 'It is sandwiched between two major civilizations' (China and India); 'The Tibetan culture is a culture sandwiched in-between, but it has its particularity in geography'; complemented with statements such as 'the Tibetans on the one hand absorbed a lot of Buddhist culture from India'; 'The Han civilization and other important civilizations have been embedded in the entire Tibetan traditional culture system'. Referring to the contacts with the outside world during the Tang dynasty (618–907), he refers to keywords suggesting intercultural encounters: 'intermarriage, cultural exchanges, and translate lots of Chinese literature'.

Somewhat similar arguments are also shared by the Chinese Korean scholar, although his timeline appears to be shorter. The scholar focuses on the issues of culture and identity in his description of Minzu. After mentioning a book that he has written about Minzu policy and the Korean Minzu, the participant tells of the history of this Minzu, which he describes as a 'cross-border and migration Minzu'. He then makes a statement about the fact that Chinese Koreans have specific cultural characteristics:

Excerpt 2

Although the culture is still very similar to the culture of North Korea and South Korea, it has formed some unique cultural characteristics in the process of communicating, absorbing and merging with China's cultural and national conditions. To sum up, in terms of the Minzu history, it originated from the Korean nation, but from the perspective of present state, it is a Minzu living in Chinese society and land, so it has its own realistic and unique characteristics.

Hybridity between a 'border' identity (North/South Korea) and the Chinese identity, as we shall see later, is often commented upon by the participants. This process is constructed here by the use of three verbs: *communicating*, *absorbing* and *merging with*. Following this statement, the scholar divides this Minzu into two groups: 'older Korean people' and 'the young people', who, in terms of identity feel the same towards their double identities, with a slight difference:

Excerpt 3

For some older Korean people, they may miss their hometown because most of them were born in the Korean Peninsula, but at the same time, they think they are Chinese already. For the young people, most of them think they are Chinese Koreans, and they also admit the fact that their ancestors migrated from the Korean Peninsula several years ago. Therefore, the concept that Chinese Koreans' national identity is not strong is wrong.

Through comparing these two groups and giving them generic voices ('they may miss . . . they think they are . . . they also admit . . .'), the scholar is able to draw a conclusion at the end of his turn, questioning the 'common-sense' idea that Chinese Koreans don't feel their Chinese national identity strongly.

The Bouyei scholar also goes back in history and mentions a book he published in English to introduce his Minzu to people outside China.

Unlike the Tibetan and Korean scholars, he comments on the complexity of who the Bouyei came to be historically:

Excerpt 4

Most of the academic circles agree that the Bouyei Minzu has developed from the ancient Baiyue branch, namely the Luoyue, and people in some parts of Western Europe also originated from a certain Baiyue branch. Because the South is an area where several Minzus live together and there are Pu in the South, some scholars think Bouyei Minzu is the Pu but those scholars who study Gelao Minzu don't agree. They think Pu is the Gelao.

In this excerpt, debates between scholars as to who the Bouyei are, especially in terms of origins, are described by the scholar. He uses different labels to translate the confusion as to who their ancestors were: the Luoyue and/or the Pu, tribes that inhabited parts of South China and northern Vietnam in the past. By so doing, he shares with us an important conversation about Chinese Minzus and the controversial issue of classification. It is claimed, for instance, that the Bouyei and the Zhuang share the same original ancestry (Shi et al., 2011).

For the Zhuang scholar, discussing the notion of Minzu with foreigners involves problematizing the relations between 'minority' Minzus and the Han majority. The Zhuang and Han peoples are described as similar, based on their agricultural background:

Excerpt 5

The Han nationality is an agricultural nation. Agricultural Minzus have generally similar psychological profiles. The Zhuang nationality is also an agricultural Minzu. Of course, the Han Minzu is a kind of agricultural Minzu in the Han region. Wheat is the main species, and the Zhuang Minzu cultivates rice. They are both agriculture-based, so the Zhuang Minzu is easier to get influenced by Confucian views.

For the scholar, their agricultural background revolves around an emphasis on wheat for the Han people and rice for the Zhuang. Through this similarity – which seems in a sense to essentialize the two groups – the scholar asserts that the Zhuang were more easily influenced by Confucianism (from the philosopher Confucius 551–479 BCE), a worldview said to be shared by the Han majority (Cheng, 2007).

For the Yi scholar, the emphasis is on particularism and differential-ism to describe the Minzu to foreigners. First, he discusses the historical background to the Yi Minzu, going back to the Xia and Shang Dynasties (2070–1046 BCE) and discussing their common origins with another Minzu, the Bai Minzu based today in the Yunnan, Guizhou and Hunan Provinces. However, he then focuses on the specificities of the Yi in cultural and linguistic terms and mentions:

Excerpt 6

Since our Minzu has a relatively long history, it has its own culture. The first thing in the culture is astronomy, and then we have our own calendar. The Yi people are different from the others. Their wisdom is very high. And then it has its own medicine, then its own writing and language, and until today it has its own.

The choice of qualifiers is of interest since they seem to put forward strong, original and (maybe) Minzu-centric aspects of the Yi: 'relatively long' (history), 'very high' (wisdom) and the repetition of 'own' (culture, calendar, medicine, language).

The last point of this section, where the participants describe the idea of Minzu and/or their own Minzu to (imagined) foreigners, takes place through a comparison between Minzu and Western diversity politics. The Hui scholar makes this comparison. From the beginning of his interview, the scholar explains that the notion of Minzu cannot be compared to issues of ethnicity in the 'West'. The scholar first spends some minutes discussing the confusion triggered by the use of words in Chinese and English that don't have the same connotations such as *ethnicity*, *nation* and *country*. He then comes to his main point to explain what Minzu is about:

Excerpt 7

In China, ethnic policy is a political system, and the constitution clearly states the system of Minzu regional autonomy. Our policies are linked to politics, economy and culture. We believe that Minzu are political, economic and cultural. Western countries only recognize the cultural aspects of minorities. Some of our scholars say they want to 'depoliticize' and think they are successful, but they are not. The resistance of black Americans has lasted for two or three hundred years. Has it succeeded? Chinese ethnic policies have only been a few decades, and if something happens, it feels that foreign systems are good, and China is bad, so some Chinese scholars think that we must learn from them to 'depoliticize' and put forward the view that 'a Minzu is a cultural group and has nothing to do with politics'.

In this excerpt, the scholar problematizes Minzu versus ethnicity debates in the West by claiming that, while Minzu discussions and actions are essentially political in China (e.g. Autonomous Regions, preferential policies), the West has focused mostly on cultural aspects of ethnicity ('cultural rights'). He also mentions the controversy launched by Ma Rong (2017), a professor at a top university in Beijing, about 'depoliticizing' Minzu to focus on cultural aspects of it (see 'some of our scholars say they want'), to which he clearly disagrees and disparages in what follows:

Excerpt 8

In fact, my opinion is that without politics, there is nothing, and the fundamental power is political power. What is politics? What do politicians do? It is for power. Without politics, can you get economic benefits? Can culture be developed? Do you have that chance? Others are in control. Why do you say you want to develop your culture? The surface is given to you, but in fact you can't develop it.

His view appears to be clearly expressed here and he uses indirect questions (with a generic *you* addressed to an 'imaginary' Minzu) to support it. Without political power and/or representation, for this scholar, there is no economic and cultural development. This is, according to the scholar, the main difference.

In the rest of his answer, the scholar insists on the differences between China and other 'foreign countries' to justify his arguments – and thus emphasizes the explanation of Minzu in political terms. This also leads him to criticize foreigners for both not understanding Chinese views on internal ethnic relations and imposing their views on the Middle Kingdom:

Excerpt 9

They don't understand China's history and national conditions. Some politicians or scholars know a little bit more deeply, and those who are hostile will say, 'You are not right, you have to learn like us, or you have to be "one nation is a country", nations have the right to self-determination, and nations have the right to build their own country.' So they support Uyghurs, engage in East Turkistan and Tibet engages in Tibet independence. Then our scholars feel wrong, saying that we should downplay the ethnic boundaries, so that no one will engage in division.

In this excerpt, the Hui scholar uses represented discourses of the voices of 'imagined' foreigners to share their misjudgments about Chinese Minzu ethnic politics. In the coda of this turn, he asserts that this often leads Chinese scholars ('our' scholars) to support more cultural views of Minzu relations versus political ones – to mimic the 'Other' and to avoid being judged by them. In the interview, the same scholar even goes as far as sharing his own disagreement with these scholars – hinting at the case of Ma from Peking University again:

Excerpt 10

I have a different view from the professor of sociology at Peking University. We won't attack each other even though we think quite differently. And I didn't debate issues with others. Even if I disagree with them I just say my views. One of the professors at Peking University is specialized in political sciences. He is a commentator. He said: 'I learned political science from the United States. Americans said that citizens are equal, but American political scientists also know that citizens have never been equal, and there will never be equality between citizens in this society.'

What he does in this excerpt is criticize indirectly this other professor for being too influenced by American ideologies of ethnic relations, and to be made to believe, in a sense, that equality is possible, if political aspects are removed (see Ma, 2017 and Zhang & Chen, 2014 about this controversy).

In this first section, we have seen a variety of perspectives on Minzu as presented to foreigners. History, especially from an intercultural perspective, particularism/differentialism and political versus culturalizing discourses of Minzu constitute the core of the scholars' descriptions of the idea of Minzu. Figure 1.2 highlights the tensions that we have identified in the scholars' discourses.

Fluidity of Minzus: trans-border/national, simplexity and translanguaging

Minzu, through politics, culture and language, was characterized by fluidity in the previous section (see the tensions in Figure 1.2). Three keywords are used here to summarize how the Minzu specialists qualify the fluidity of Minzu (see Figure 1.3): trans-border/trans-nationalism (most Minzus are located on the borders between China and other countries, as asserted before, historically this means cultural-linguistic interactions), simplexity (a term borrowed from Berthoz (2010) to refer to the simplex-complex continuum of cultural diversity, that is, simple solutions found to prepare an action and plan for the consequences of complexity) and translanguaging

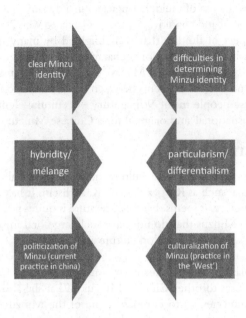

Figure 1.2 Tensions in determining Minzu

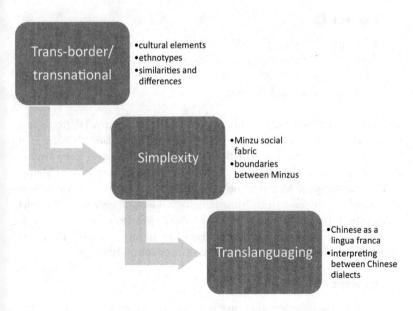

Figure 1.3 Fluidity of Minzus

(defined here as the use of multiple languages in a dynamic process to navigate complex social and cognitive demands, Garcia & Wei, 2014).

The first aspect of fluidity that is highlighted by many of the scholars is the trans-border/transnational characteristic of Minzu. The Kirgiz scholar specializes in the 'Epic of Manas', an epic poem transmitted orally revolving around a series of events between the Kyrgyz people with Turkic and Chinese people in the 9th century – a cultural element that she defines as 'transnational' and original for a Chinese Minzu:

Excerpt 11

It belongs to transnational culture, including several countries in Central Asia, such as Kyrgyzstan and Kazakhstan. It has a great influence. Therefore, it seems that folk literature is quite special compared with other Minzus that do not have such large oral implementation or have no great influence on culture and art.

What the scholar does here is create a transnational identity for her Minzu which she opposes to other Chinese Minzus. What she also seems to be doing in the interview is to compare some of the Minzus close to the Kirgiz Minzu, to other transnational peoples. She refers to ethnotypes (references to physical attributes) to compare them (Lafont, 1971):

Excerpt 12

Sometimes Uygur people look like Turks. You can't tell them clearly. They have a high nose and European origins. Their noses are quite wide on this side. And then they look at them with a special preference for Indians and Pakistanis.

The cross-border (transnational) aspect of Minzu identity, language and culture is also emphasized by the Hui scholar who explains that the Hui usually speak Chinese but that they use words and phrases from Arabic and Persian, especially when they deal with religious matters (e.g. Islam).

This transnational Minzu identity is further discussed by the Mongolian scholar, when he refers to their Minzu language. The Chinese Inner Mongolia Autonomous Region is located on the border to Mongolia (Монгол Улс ; capital: Ulaanbaatar), which shares a lot of similarities with Chinese Mongolians. The scholar explains about their common language:

Excerpt 13

In fact, the language they use is almost the same, and the main difference is the text. Mongolia (the country) uses Cyrillic Mongolian

(基里尔斯拉夫蒙古文), and we (Inner Mongolia of China) use the ancient Uighur Mongolian (回鹘式蒙古文), so the use of characters is the fundamental difference. In addition, in terms of language, Mongolia's language is more unified, and almost everyone speaks Mongolian. However, most people in Inner Mongolia probably speak Chinese, and only a few people really speak or understand Mongolian.

The scholar notes two main differences 'trans-borderly': in terms of how Mongolian is written (influences from Russia in Mongolia where it is written in the Cyrillic alphabet; Inner Mongolia uses the traditional script, which is traditionally written in vertical lines) and in the amount of people who can speak the language on either side of the border, with Chinese Mongolians using mostly Mandarin Chinese:

Excerpt 14

As far as culture is concerned, Inner Mongolia retains some traditional cultures better than Mongolia. Because Mongolia was influenced by the Soviet Union, its Westernization was serious.

In cultural terms, the scholar notes the differences between these two trans-border Mongolias in relation to Chinese and Russian influences. Referring to the different linguistic use and the influence of the Chinese and Russian languages, the scholar mentions two examples: the words *tractor* and *communism* – while in Mongolia people use the Russian words for these two terms, in Chinese Mongolian, they use their own Mongolian words. Interestingly the scholar ends his discussion of this difference by claiming that the two places 'are different in language and vocabulary, but not in culture' – an assertion he does not develop.

The second aspect of this section is simplexity (the enmeshment of simplicity and complexity in Minzu fluidity). The Bouyei explicates the complex social fabric of Minzus throughout the country, using his own Minzu as an example:

Excerpt 15

I(nterviewer): Mr. XX, I know that there are Dong Minzu, Miao Minzu, Gelao Minzu and your minority – Bouyei Minzu in Guizhou. These minorities all live together, right?
R(espondent): The Bouyei Minzu mainly lives together with the Miao Minzu.
I: What are the differences between the culture of Bouyei Minzu and Miao Minzu?

R: Miao culture and Bouyei culture are quite different, because they do not belong to the same language group. In ethnological terms, Miao Minzu and Bouyei Minzu belong to different ethnic groups. Each ethnic minority group has its own national costumes with distinctive features. But from the appearance of their clothes, there is no difference between the clothes of Gelao Minzu and the clothes of Han Minzu. Not only does Gelao Minzu lose its characteristic national clothes, but its Minzu language also almost dies out. The Number of Bouyei in Guizhou is very few. The Bouyei Minzu in Guizhou live together with the Miao Minzu, the Bouyei Minzu in the west live together with the Yi Minzu, and the Bouyei Minzu in the east live together with the Shui Minzu. The Dong Minzu is far away from us, so there is little crossover.

This excerpt contains a conversation between one of us and the scholar about interminzu relations with his group. The interviewer guides the conversation around the potential similarities between the participant's Minzu and other ones – using the key concept of *culture* as a determinant for evaluating difference (see the problems in doing so in e.g. Holliday, 2010). The participant's answer emphasizes the complexity of these relations and potential similarities. The only Minzus that appear to share such similarities are the Gelao and the majority Han, because the former has lost 'its characteristic national clothes' and its own language has almost disappeared. What this excerpt shows is that groups in different regions and areas of China have different relations with, and opportunities to meet, each other.

The Bouyei scholar continues his panorama of interminzu relations, urged by the interviewer to comment on language use. When asked what language the Bouyei speak, the scholar mentions Zhuang. Then follows a long conversation about language difference, similarity and forms of translanguaging:

Excerpt 16

I: If one person speaks Zhuang language, how much can you understand?

R: It depends on what region the person is from.

I: What if they are from Wuming?[2]

R: I can't understand the Zhuang language in Wuming area, because it is very different from Bouyei language. But I can understand the Zhuang words of areas like Tianlin[3] and so on.

Q: How much can you understand? 50 per cent?

R: I can understand 80 per cent.

Q: Can you understand 80 per cent? Why?
R: Because the Zhuang language in these areas has a lot of the same vocabulary as Bouyei.

Zhuang is in fact a complex set of more than 12 languages spoken in the South of China, which are not mutually intelligible (Handel, 2019). This shows again that the borders between Minzus are not always clear-cut and that complexity and hybridity seem to be strong components of what they are from cultural and linguistic perspectives.

In terms of similarities and differences, it is actually interesting to see that the scholar argues that 'sometimes it is difficult to communicate with one's own ethnic group, but it is easier to communicate with neighboring ethnic groups'. When asked to exemplify, he mentions the fact the Zhuang from Xining in the Qinghai Province (Central China) may not understand Zhuang from Wuming (South China) while they may understand the Bouyei Minzu language.

This point is actually illustrated by the Zhuang specialist. When asked about communication between Zhuang people, he starts by explaining that there are at least 12 different dialects of Zhuang in China and that they are not mutually intelligible. As a bridge, the specialist asserts that 'in general, communication between different Zhuang native-speaking regions takes place in the Southwest of China and in Guangdong, and relatively few Minzu languages are used'.

Interestingly, the Tibetan scholar notes a somewhat similar phenomenon when he describes communication between Han people themselves. Putonghua ('Standard Mandarin') is the common language, the lingua franca used in China. This language has many dialects, which are also not necessarily mutually intelligible. The scholar recounts something he observed during a visit in Quanzhou, southern Fujian, beside the Taiwan Strait:

Excerpt 17

For the first time, I saw a Han Chinese serving as an interpreter for a Han Chinese, they speak Hokkien dialect and our delegation went there. Teacher XXX has some cooperation projects with us. He invited us to Quanzhou to have a meeting. After we were finished, we went to visit a small temple. The old man in the temple, a thin and tall man, was very knowledgeable and he was very familiar with things, but he could not speak Mandarin. He explained to us, except for Teacher XXX and two or three other people, we couldn't understand a word. Later, the curator of a local museum did the interpreting for us. The old man spoke in Minnan dialect, and he translated it into Mandarin. Han people act as interpreters for the Han people, my God!

As a minority Minzu, the scholar was surprised that the Han Minzu also had to use an alternative way of communicating with each other beyond the language that they share.

This section has dealt with Minzu as a symbol of fluidity and presented three perspectives on this aspect: trans-/border/nationalism, simplexity and translanguaging. What this section also emphasizes is the centrality and complexity of interminzu relations. The next section explores this topic based on what the scholars shared with us.

Qualifying interminzu relations

In this third and last section we look into the way the specialists discuss aspects of interminzu encounters and communication. In general, they refer to phenomena of inclusiveness, co-influence and historical perspectives. These represent answers to the question of what the world could learn from interminzu communication, as was asked during the interviews.

Qualifying interminzu relations starts with political versus intercultural perspectives – although the border between these two aspects is not always clear (see e.g. Dervin & Simpson, 2021). Let us start exploring the political with the Han Minzu scholar, who often compartmentalizes Chinese Minzus. In this excerpt, he tells us that Minzu groups can be divided into anthropological categories of 'farming, nomadic, Mountain Minzus'. He adds: 'some are semi-agricultural and semi-nomadic, pure nomadic'. Based on these anthropological categories, which have been highly criticized in recent years (see Kaufman, 2009) he comments on the different groups' abilities or un/willingness to be in contact with others:

Excerpt 18

For example, compared with other Minzu groups, nomadic peoples have a higher degree of openness, but affected by the geographical environment, farming Minzu groups, such as the mountain Minzu groups in Yunnan, Guizhou and Sichuan, and those living in remote mountainous areas are less open to the outside world.

His claim is then related to discussions of 'development': the more developed, the more willing a Minzu is to communicate with others and to 'get out of their original environment'. Since 1949 (the birth of the People's Republic of China), the scholar explains that all Minzu groups have been able and urged to work and live with other groups. The Han scholar is a specialist of Ethnic Ethics and has done work on Minzu myths, legends, folk tales and heroic epics. He mentions *The Epic of King Gesar* of the Tibetan Minzu (dating back to the 12th century), and the aforementioned *Epic of Manas* of the Kirgiz, which he claims are very close to the Core Socialist Values of China from 2012, which include values such as *prosperity*, *democracy* and *freedom* (Cheng, 2007). His conclusion consists in saying that:

Excerpt 19

Therefore, we must integrate the cultures of all ethnic groups to promote the core socialist values among all ethnic groups. The traditional culture of the nation is absorbed from the traditional virtues, and then it can be further deepened.

In a similar vein, the Hui scholar also divides the Minzu groups into categories when he discusses their abilities to interact with and learn from each other:

Excerpt 20

Mongolians graze on the grasslands. They live like that. Their lifestyle and culture are more adaptable than others. Fishermen are on the sea, and other inland people can't do that. Their kind of culture has led to a way of production, lifestyle and interpersonal relationship, so that they can fish on the sea. Therefore, the variety of cultures should be developed and retained and given opportunities for development. Every culture has backward parts and dross, including those of the Han, so we must always abandon the dross, keep the useful and modern social development and keep it for development and must be done continuously. There are also many useless things, feudal superstitions. Everyone has to move towards a modern society.

Using the opposed examples of Mongolians and 'fishermen' the participant claims that they have different ways and opportunities for dialoguing with others. However, he notes that certain aspects of Minzu cultures (e.g. 'useless things', superstitions) could be discarded so as to keep positive elements ('useful and modern social development') and move towards 'modern' (economic?) development.

Interestingly, the scholar concludes his turn by emphasizing the importance for China (and Chinese Minzus) to learn from the outside world in terms of relations:

Excerpt 21

Not only with the 56 Minzus in China, we also have to learn from foreign countries. Not only do we learn from each other in China, but how much we learn from Westerners, and even learn from them every day.

The outside world here means *foreign countries*, which are turned into *Westerners*. The idea of learning from the 'West' – rather than with – has strongly influenced Chinese scholarship since the end of the 19th century (Cheng, 2007).

In the next excerpt, intercultural aspects of interminzu relations are discussed. In so doing, the Bouyei scholar starts by defining the Bouyei people as 'simple and kind, good at communication, highly tolerant' – a definition that appears to be both generic and Minzu-centric. He then describes a custom that both illustrates and shows how this applies to interminzu interrelations:

Excerpt 22

R: For example, if I am 15 years old, I will find a male of Han Minzu or Miao Minzu or other Minzu of the same age to become good friends with him. This is called sworn brothers between boys and blood sisters between girls.

Q: Does it mean to find a bestie?

R: That's right.

Q: This happens between people, right?

R: This is usually done between different Minzu groups. During festivals like the Spring Festival, sworn followers will be invited to their homes. If they have any difficulties, we will offer help.

Q: Why would you do that?

R: This is a custom of communication. For example, if someone has a son who is in poor health, they should find a godfather for him from another Minzu group.

In this series of turns, the interviewer and the scholar negotiate the meaning of the 'sworn brothers and sisters' tradition (結拜), which creates some form of Godparent relations between people of different Minzus (e.g. Bouyei + Han/Miao). In his study of a Miao village, Wang (2018: 62) describes what 'sworn brother-/sister-hood' consists in:

all sworn brothers come to give a hand for carrying firewood, while the housewife prepares a feast for coming brothers and their wives. They sit around eating, talking, laughing and playing porker until midnight. The gathering makes both cooperation among sworn brothers and progression emotion each other.

This habit is qualified as 'a basis for national unity' by the Bouyei scholar, which he confirms by claiming that 'This custom would not exist if Minzu groups did not believe in each other'. This Minzu inclusiveness from the Bouyei side is also illustrated by the scholar's claim that Minzus learn each other's language to be able to interact with each other:

Excerpt 23

We learn the languages of other peoples in order to acquire a life skill of communicating with them. It is not surprising, for example, that Han people living in the Bouyei Minzu region are generally fluent in the Bouyei language, and that Bouyei people can also speak Chinese. In this way, there will be no misunderstandings between different Minzus because of language barriers. When I can speak your Minzu language, there is no barrier between us.

This somewhat idealistic qualification of interminzu relations ('When I can speak your Minzu language, there is no barrier between us') emphasizes however the importance of language learning and use for intergroup relations.

The Korean scholar is also very positive about his own Minzu's ability to interact with other Minzus. He asserts:

Excerpt 24

The Korean group actually has a good relationship with others, especially with Han group, that's why Yanbian has become the model of Autonomous Prefecture for many years and the advanced model of national unity for six years. Korean ethnic group does a good job in getting along well with other groups. I think it will continue in the future.

When urged to explain why the Korean group is good at creating positive encounters with others, he shares the opinion that it is able to both 'accept other Minzus' cultures and to keep its own culture'. The scholar develops the following argument:

Excerpt 25

Actually, it accepts a lot of culture of Han. Korean ethnic group is different from some groups, one of which is Man, which lost its culture after being exposed to other cultures. However, Korean ethnic group can keep its cultural characteristics. Meanwhile, it accepts and respects other groups' culture, so it's very easy for others to communicate with it. Assuming that Korean ethnic group had totally accepted the culture of Han and invited people of Han to celebrate their festivals, it was very likely for people of Han to feel bored because there were no differences between their ways of observing festivals and Koreans'. From this, we can say a group should keep its own culture because the culture may attract people from other ethnic groups.

In this excerpt, the scholar starts by comparing the situation of the Korean Minzu and that of the Manchu Minzu, whose 'language' and 'culture' have vanished, and who have become 'Han' in a sense. He then argues that by keeping some of its cultural characteristics, the Korean Minzu is appealing to other Minzus, especially to the Han Minzu. The coda of the excerpt summarizes the main argument of his turn: keeping one's culture is a way of creating interminzu interrelation.

A very similar argument is shared by the Tibetan scholar, although he approaches the issue from a different perspective. For him, all Minzus have something to bring to the table, 'culturally' speaking. However, he adds that each Minzu needs to learn about other Minzus to enrich their own lives. This is how he formulates this idea:

Excerpt 26

You have to jump out of your own culture, right? Then you can look back. If a person cannot jump out of a cultural tradition, you also have a poor understanding of the culture itself. You must jump out of Tibetan culture. Especially when you look at those different cultures, you can't see a lot of things, right?

Using a generic 'you' (and repeating phrases such as 'jump out of your own culture'), and constructing some kind of imaginary dialogue, he makes claims about the necessity to look at oneself from the outside while acquainting oneself with other cultures – an argument that is omnipresent in the intercultural education literature, see Abdallah-Pretceille (2004). He also gives several examples of how he has himself promoted this attitude amongst his Tibetan friends and colleagues:

Excerpt 27

I encouraged some very good teachers to read books from other Minzu groups. Don't read Tibetan all the time. They are all Tibetan teachers with only one knowledge system. You have to jump out your own culture circle. So, I sent one or two young teachers to study at a Minzu College [in the South of China], finally they get their Doctor's degree. Later, I encouraged some students to continue their studies and then introduced them to Peking University [a top university in Beijing]. When you are in the Han circle, you can look at the way the Han people think and their knowledge system.

The scholar also insists on learning from the 'West' and explains that he has sent some Minzu students to the USA (Harvard University), Germany (Humbolt), Italy (Naples Oriental University) and so on (see Cheng's 2007 idea of the constant intellectual motorway between the West and China).

Figure 1.4 summarizes the political and intercultural ideological components of the participants' discourses about interminzu relations. As asserted at the beginning of this section, the border between the political and the intercultural tends to be ambiguous at times since the way relations are perceived is always enmeshed in both perspectives (see Piller, 2010). We argue, however, that both can inform us of the ideas circulating around interminzu relations in China.

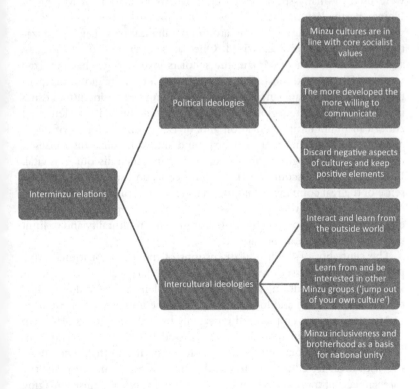

Figure 1.4 Interminzu relations

[Pause]

In this chapter we were interested in exploring further the idea of Chinese Minzu as a potential original entry point and as a complement and companion to, for example, bilingual, multicultural and intercultural education. We have noted that current scientific discussions about the notion both in China and elsewhere appear to be confused and confusing and that there is a need to make it more comprehensible and meaningful if it is to be taken seriously.

Based on interviews with interdisciplinary experts from a university specializing in Chinese Minzu, we have discussed: 1 How they construct Minzu for the outside world; 2 How they determine Minzu fluidity by considering trans/border-national, simplex and linguistic issues; 3 How they qualify interminzu relations.

For the first aspect, we noted both similarities and differences in the way they describe Minzus to outsiders ('foreigners' in the interviews): (complex) intercultural (short- and long-term-) historical perspectives were used by many specialists to describe the formation of Minzus in China; particularism/differentialism but also similarities and merging were described while the debate around culturalization versus politicization of Minzu was problematized. One can see that in order to present and discuss the idea of Minzu, the scholars give a somewhat localized vision of Chinese 'ethnic' issues, while relating it to more global perspectives. This is important since discussions of inter- and multicultural issues in education are often globalized and visualized through the lenses of American multicultural education and/or Europeanized forms of intercultural education. In order to diversify and 'interculturalize' discourses of diversity education, glocalizing/recontextualizing such discourses is vital. In the specialists' discourses (who are not education specialists) we get a sense of the real complexity and multifacetedness of the narratives around Minzu. Becoming aware of this complexity might help those involved in education to open up new discussions around interculturality and to limit stereotyping what Minzu is about.

The centrality of fluidity in discussions of transborder-national, simplex and linguistic issues was obvious. The specialists described well the importance of considering Minzu through this lens and to explore its historical, transnational and local perspectives. The importance of language in Minzu issues was emphasized repeatedly by the different scholars – an aspect which is often ignored in Minzu studies and/or the writings of Western scholars about Minzu in education. This means that, when dealing with diversity education, using Minzu as a lens, we need to take the three aspects of transborder-transnational, simplexity and translanguaging into account to raise, for example, students' awareness of the complexity of intercultural issues in education.

Finally, the study of the specialists' discourses demonstrates that, as far as interminzu communication is concerned, there are, on the one hand, certain ideologies that could be considered as politically specific to the Chinese context (e.g. 'the more developed, the more willing to communicate'), while others could be labelled as interculturally ideological (e.g. 'jump out of your own culture'). Although the second set of ideologies might be more familiar to people from outside China, again, the first set reminds us that we need to bear in mind local conditions and discourses, and not quickly disparage or criticize them. Political ideologies about diversity from the 'Western' world can also often be considered problematic. In educational terms, such as when working with student teachers, we need to train them to separate these ideologies and to see if some of these ideologies can serve the purpose of making intercultural education more inclusive of other ideologies. It is also important to perform discourse analyses of more politically oriented discourses so that student teachers can become aware of the influence that politics has on the way they are made to think about it.

Exploring the complexities of Minzu as a companion and contribution to global discussions of interculturality in education – while refraining from stereotyping and limiting what it entails – is important in a world of research that tends to be monological. In order to build up counternarratives to Western-centric epistemologies there is a need to explore other contexts again and again. Looking into interdisciplinary discourses, we argue, can also give us opportunities to obtain both a fine-grained but also complex picture of a fabric of diversity discourses.

[Time to reflect]

- The experts held a diverse range of ideas and views about Chinese Minzu. Which ones do you find inspiring, challenging and/or problematic, and why?
- How aware are you of the influence of political and economic views on the way interculturality is taught and discussed in your own context? What position(s) do local vs. more global politics and economy have in these views?
- In this chapter there are clear hints that personal and political beliefs do influence the way we talk about and 'do' diversity and interculturality. One's own position as a member of a

group always has an impact on how we perceive interculturality as an object of research/education. Can you state what influences you in the way you understand interculturality? What about your friends? Your teachers?

- Consider the way the society you live in functions in terms of interculturality (majority–minority, migrants, etc.). Go back to Figure 1.2 and try to put on paper the tensions that this society witnesses.
- What role do cross-border interactions play in your context? How are they included in discourses of interculturality in education?

Notes

1 'All nationalities have the freedom to use and develop their own spoken and written languages and to preserve or reform their own folkways and customs.'
2 Located in the capital of the Guangxi Zhuang Autonomous Region (South China).
3 County in the west of Guangxi.

2 Specificities of Minzu education

In Chinese philosophy, learning and education have always held a central position. The teacher has also represented an important figure. In the third and fourth centuries AD, the brief essay of Confucian teachings, 学记 (*Xueji, On Teaching and Learning*) from 礼记 (*Liji, On Rites*), presented the most important principles of education and pedagogy. In 学记 education in Ancient Chinese politics was also revered: 'when establishing states and governing the people, [Ancient kings] made instruction and schools a primary object'. Throughout her history, but especially since the proclamation of the birth of the People's Republic of China by Chairman Mao Zedong in 1949, China has paid attention to sharing her passion for education with all Chinese citizens, regardless of where they are located in the country and of their Minzu. As such, as asserted in the previous chapter, preferential policies are implemented in China to improve the socio-economic and educational development of all Minzus, especially those in border regions. To expand, in terms of education, boarding schools, preferential admissions and remedial programs are put into action. Noteworthy is the fact that the Chinese Ministry of Education comprises a department of ethnic minority education. The decade-long scholarship on Minzu education locally and internationally is also a testimony to China's serious interest in the idea of 'education for all' (Yuan et al., 2020).

Recently Amsler et al. (2020, p. 13) have been critical of the overly Western flavour of, for example, multicultural and intercultural education around the world and call for a move 'beyond existing frameworks of modernist knowledge, politics and economic systems'. Dealing with diversity in education has been approached in multiple ways around the world. Although we are said to live in a 'global world', a given ideology ('ought to be', the 'taken for granted') relates to a specific context, especially in its economic-political outlook. When using 'Americano-centric'

DOI: 10.4324/9781351044554-3

ideologies about diversity in education, there is a need to pay attention to the connotations and consequences on our research. As such, the use of e.g. Banks' (1989) work on multicultural education can be problematic in the Chinese context since it discusses issues of diversity which are not at the core of Minzu issues in education (e.g. the concept of race). This does not mean that we should ignore or get rid of these ideologies. As Liu et al. (2020: 280) note rightly: 'Studies developed in the Western context are useful in understanding non-Western contexts as they provide researchers with an initial perspective and a framework to approach the multicultural education field.'

While some localized forms of alternative, complementary and companion education have been identified (e.g. *interculturalidad* in South America, *interculturalité* in France, *tabunka kyōsei* ('multiculturalism and coexistence') in Japan), some ideological perspectives have dominated worldwide, albeit in different modes. This is the case of such approaches as (American) multicultural education (e.g. Banks, 1989) and (European) Intercultural Education (e.g. Grant & Portera, 2010). In the Chinese context, American multicultural education has often been used to frame and conceptualize Minzu education since the 1980s.

Minzu education is a label that does not refer to any unified approach to interculturality in education in China. In this chapter, it refers to formal and informal aspects of Chinese education, related in/directly to Minzu. Different models of Minzu education have been identified in the literature. First, some Minzu groups can be educated in their home provinces in their first language, in Putonghua or in both languages (Leibold & Chen, 2014). Second, three different types of primary and secondary schools are available: mono-ethnic Minzu schools, mixed Minzu schools, and mixed Han/other Minzu schools. Top students from Tibet and Xinjiang can also receive their middle and high school education in Putonghua in other provinces (so-called 'inland' education). Leibold (2016) thus argues that China has the world's most extensive regime of minority affirmative action policies or 'preferential policies' (优惠政策) in terms of admission to educational institutions and employment in state or public institutions, acknowledging the existence of educational inequality.

In their review of what they call 'Chinese multicultural education', Zhang and Chen (2014) note the following specificities:

- In Chinese citizenship education the centrality of both national and Minzu identities is emphasized. Strengthening all citizens' Chinese national identity (like in most other countries, see e.g. the idea of

citizenship education in Europe) is deemed essential to ensure social cohesion.
- Minority cultural and linguistic teaching is made available to Minzu students who have a first language other than Standard Chinese.
- School culture and as many teaching activities as possible should integrate students' cultural backgrounds and experiences in basic education.

Theoretically, there have been attempts at problematizing and conceptualizing Minzu education. However, there is no unified theoretical underpinning of Minzu education in China, apart from the notion of 'plurality within unity', which relates Chinese national unity and Minzu diversity. Chinese students tend to experience diversity in terms of language, culture, and sometimes worldview/religion. Their identity thus can be situated on a continuum of Chineseness and Minzu (see Yang's (2017) study on different Tibetan students' identification). Xing (2001: 580–581) is one of the few scholars to have tried to devise an 'integrated multicultural education' containing both 'plurality within unity' and (American) multicultural education (following American scholars like Banks). The development of Minzus in China (culturally, economically, educationally and politically) has also been problematized by means of a 'sinicized' version of Marxist ethnic theory (Jin et al., 2012). As such, MUC which is referred to many times in this book, teaches the theory, ideology and politics of China's ethnic policies and the 'solving of China's ethnic problems' (Clothey & Hu, 2014).

In 1988 anthropologist Fei Xiaotong published the oft-quoted paper 'The Chinese Nation with Multi-ethnic Groups' which contains a macro-theory of the formation and structural characteristics of the Chinese nation. His main analytical element of China as a unified multi-ethnic country is summarized in the phrase 一体多元 (*yiti duoyuan, united but pluralistic*). Today, Fei's theory has been adopted by both education policy-makers and scholars in China under the label 'unified pluralist education' (多元一体教育, *duoyuan yiti jiaoyu*).

It is important to note that in terms of teaching, Minzu education concerns both specific forms of educational approaches (e.g. meeting the needs of Minzu students, bilingual education, Minzu higher education institutions) and education for all (e.g. teaching aspects of Minzu included in e.g. moral and political education in basic education).

Several Chinese scholars have created and designed a specific approach to Chinese Minzu education which they label as 'integrated multicultural education' (see Teng, 2010). At the core of this perspective lies unity education, based on Fei's (1988) theory of plural unity pattern. Through this aspect Minzu students learn about their own Minzu's origins, history of formation and development while reflecting on the fact that their Minzu is interrelated with other Chinese Minzus through a common sense of national belongingness. Minzu education theories such as 'integrated multicultural education' proposed by Teng (2010) were also directly inspired by Fei's work. The aims of this approach are to promote common economic development, cultural heritage, cross-cultural communication, the political equality of all Minzu groups, and the ultimate realization of national unity (Teng, 2010). In 2012 Teng described his approach as follows:

> the education of a multi-ethnic country has the function not only to transfer the common human cultural achievements, but also, it should pass on the valued and time-honored cultural traditions of its dominant ethnic group as well as the ethnic minorities.

For the educationalist these concern all students in all Chinese schools, majority Han as well as other Minzu groups. As such, Han students (and teachers) should get to know the languages and cultures of various Minzu groups too. Zhang and Chen (2014) discuss a range of policy initiatives from 1987 onwards that represents a clear shift from education for different Minzu groups to what is referred to as 'ethnic solidarity education'. This kind of education is now included in moral and patriotic education in primary and middle schools and named 'national unity education' (民族团结教育). Several textbooks are used to teach this subject and introduce students to The Big Chinese

Table 2.1 Multicultural education vs. Minzu education

Similarities	Differences
The promotion of cultural diversity	The underlying policy approach
Respecting differences between ethnic groups	Composition and habitation patterns of various ethnic groups
Developing cross-cultural teaching methods	Concerned with economic, social and cultural development
Eliminating discrimination	
Facilitating equality	
Addressing issues related to rights and political equality	

Family (primary school), Ethnic Basics (primary school) and Basics of Ethnic Policy (middle school).

Zhang and Chen (2014) remark that there are both similarities and differences between diversity education from the 'West' (multicultural/intercultural education) and Chinese Minzu perspectives. However, while multicultural education is interested in, for example, rights and political equality, Chinese Minzu education tends to put the emphasis on economic, social and cultural development. Teng and Su (1997) also explain that (Chinese) 'integrated multicultural education' can help promote cultural heritage as well as interminzu communication.

It is important to note here that the two scholars somewhat exaggerate the coherence and consistency of 'Western' multicultural education. For example, in policy and educational terms, the US and European Union do not share the same approach and values. What is more, within these entities, there might also be differences in the way discourses of *culture* are constructed (Abdallah-Pretceille, 2004). As such, in the European Union, while a country like Finland focuses on 'cultural' difference in discussions of immigration, France emphasizes 'cultural' similarity. Regardless of the 'imagined' similarities identified by the scholars, Zhang and Chen's (2014) points about differences are primordial: Chinese Minzu education is indeed based on a different policy approach ('Pluralistic Unity of the Chinese Nation' with an emphasis on difference and similarity), and its concerns have more to do with development rather than, for example, issues of political equality. Like in other countries, national identity is seen as fundamental in Chinese Minzu education to ensure social cohesion and reduce potential Minzu tensions (Qian, 2010). More importantly, Minzu groups in China are indigenous peoples unlike many of the 'targeted' populations in multicultural/intercultural education, who, for example, migrated to the US or Europe. We might want to add that multicultural and intercultural education emerged from specific historical contexts. As such, multicultural education was born out of the 1960s civil rights movements while intercultural education out of European decolonization in the 1970s. Economically and politically speaking, these differ from Chinese Minzu, whose sometimes disadvantaged position is said to derive from 'the harsh climate, undesirable geographical conditions and economic underdevelopment in the border land they occupied' (Zhang & Chen, 2014: 403). In the 'West', multicultural/intercultural education often relates to situations of education diversity in urban and large city contexts.

The basic values of Minzu education are listed in Figure 2.1:

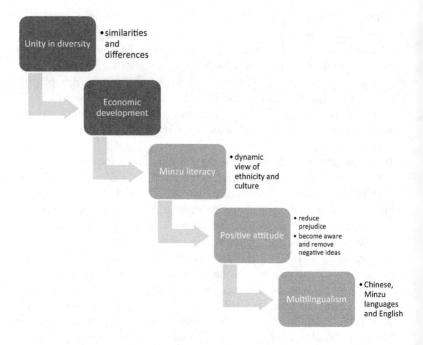

Figure 2.1 Basic values of Minzu education

Engaging with the literature published in English, we note that there is a lack of an overview of what Minzu education encompasses. Figure 2.2 represents an attempt at clarifying what this multifaceted label includes and lists perspectives that concern certain groups of students (e.g. bilingual education) and all students (e.g. national unity education).

Details are provided below about bilingual education and integrated multicultural education in teacher education.

Bilingual education plays a central part in Chinese Minzu education. Gao and Ren (2018) maintain that the 55 Minzu minority groups speak over 209 languages (e.g. Mongolian, Tibetan, Uyghur, Zhuang). In the past, Chinese scholars have noted that many Minzu students stop learning their Minzu languages because they perceive them as 'futile' in the labour market, especially when competing with other students with good Standard Chinese skills (e.g. Zenz, 2014). This has been perceived as counter to the plural unity pattern. This is why Minzu bilingual education has been put into place around the country. According to Zhou (2012), 21

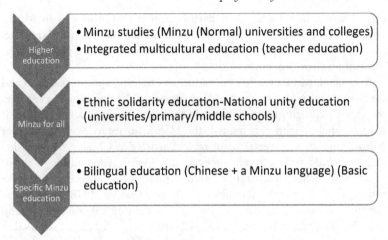

Figure 2.2 Layers of Minzu education (examples)

Minzu groups have implemented some form of bilingual education for approximately 6 million Minzu students, whereby they get to learn three languages: their first language (a Minzu language), Chinese and English. Different types of bilingual education are offered in different parts of the country (Mańkowska, 2019): 1 A Minzu language is the main language of instruction from kindergarten to middle school, with Chinese taught as a separate subject; 2 A Minzu language is used at the start of school education to help non-Chinese speakers easily understand the content. In higher grades the percentage of Minzu language teaching is reduced, and the Chinese language predominates. It is important to note that thousands of textbooks are available in Minzu languages and consist of direct translations of textbooks published in Chinese.

When it comes to teacher education and training for Minzu, few publications are available in English specifically on the way Minzu teacher education is organized. In autonomous regions of China, around 100 Minzu normal universities, normal colleges or schools for teacher education and training have been established. Some Minzu universities and colleges located in Minzu areas also offer Minzu teacher education programs. Teacher training centres have been established and Minzu teacher education courses are also widely available in major normal universities around China such as Beijing Normal University, Central China Normal University, and East China Normal University. These programs are open to both Han and non-Han students. It is also important to note that inland universities have signed partnerships with universities in Minzu areas to offer assistance in terms of Minzu teacher education and training. For instance, inland experts are sent to Minzu areas to take part in teaching and research programs.

In general, Minzu teacher education and training appears scattered and somewhat inconsistent. The emphasis appears to be on preparing teachers for specific Minzu groups rather than for mixed groups. What is more, it is often unclear who gets trained: the Han majority to work with other Minzus and/or vice versa? Most review articles of Chinese Minzu education include very few references to this specific issue although forms of Minzu teacher education and training have been organized since the founding of the People's Republic of China (Hawkins, 1978). A few articles have examined teacher education and training for teachers dealing with Minzu issues. Ou and Du's (2017) article, as an example, shows that teachers interested in strengthening students' Minzu identity can have a positive impact on their academic achievement. In her 2011 review article of a teacher education programme in the Xinjiang Uyghur Autonomous Region Liu proposes that knowledge of 'multicultural education' should be added to the curriculum. In a 2018 article about a teacher education program in Beijing Yuan shows that pre-service Han teachers were not so much in favour of specific preparation for Minzu education and were unprepared to teach about it or work in Minzu classes. Finally, in their 2014 paper entitled 'Creating a multicultural curriculum in Han-dominant schools: The policy and practice of ethnic solidarity education in China', Zhang and Chen (2014) look into teachers' preparedness to implement ethnic solidarity education in a mix of (Minzu/non-Minzu) schools in Beijing. Their findings reveal that the schools incorporated Minzu elements in the school environment, in teaching and extra-curricular activities, however the scholars note that 'they tended to focus on the static cultural artefacts, such as food, music, dance and sports etc., which represented the museum-like knowledge about different ethnic groups, i.e., the so-called "living fossil"' (Zhang & Chen, 2014: 412). 'Cultural heritage' rather than fluid and 'living' perspectives on cultural complexity was highlighted. Zhang and Chen (2014) also assert that many teachers and school leaders found ethnic solidarity education to be unneeded.

In their extensive literature review of Minzu education from 2000 to 2018, Liu et al. (2020) claim that teacher education and training for Minzu is one of the six important topics in the field. The review shows that, in general, teacher education in China seems to lack systematic and coherent Minzu perspectives. Some scholars have made suggestions as to how to strengthen this aspect of Minzu teacher preparation: Zhang (2015) emphasizes the importance of critical thinking and creative thinking; Pu and Liu (2017) insist on creating a common sense of belonging by, for example, teachers and students learning from each other through cultural exchange; Zheng (2012) suggests that teachers explore the preferred learning styles of Minzu students. Developing 'multicultural' teaching strategies is deemed to be an important option.

[Time to reflect]

- How would you summarize Chinese Minzu education in a few words? What from it seems potentially inspiring for education elsewhere?
- Is there any influential scholar or figure Fei like in your own context? What has s/he contributed to discussions of diversity and interculturality in education? Has s/he been influential outside your context?
- What do you know about these specific approaches to interculturality: *interculturalidad* (South America), *interculturalité* (France), *tabunka kyōsei* ('multiculturalism and coexistence') (Japan)? Find some background information and get acquainted with their basic principles. How do they materialize in education?
- Which levels of education include some form of intercultural education in your own context or other contexts you know well?
- Are teachers systematically trained for interculturality in the country where you reside? How?
- How do economic discourses fit into discussions of interculturality in different parts of the world? Is the word *(economic) development* used when it is discussed in your context?
- How do you understand the idea of 'cultural heritage'? How is it embedded in education in your context and other contexts you know?
- Find out about bilingual education in your context. What forms of such education are offered? Who can benefit from such education? How successful has it been in empowering bilinguals?

3   Minzu inside out

Although the notion of Minzu might be unknown to the 'West', its engagement with the world is occurring all the time. In this chapter, we focus on the phenomenon of internationalization of Minzu in higher education by analysing the perceptions of incoming international students to China.

As asserted before in this book, for many people in the world, China has represented 'traditionally the image of the ultimate Other' (Longxi, 1988: 110). Even when the Middle Kingdom is described beyond the usual monolithic image that is often applied to its 1.4 billion people (as in 'The Chinese are . . .'), its own superdiversity, or diversification of diversity (Vertovec, 2007), in terms of ethnicity, language and worldview (amongst others), often appears to be constructed in limited and limiting ways. For instance, in a 2018 article published in the *Times Higher Education*, entitled 'University Life in China', Spriggs (2018) asserts:

> China is diverse and each province has its own cultural norms, local foods, drinks and customs. With its size and reasonably cheap travel costs there is the opportunity to explore the entire country, from modern sights such as ice-cold Harbin or Shanghai's city life to ancient wonders including the Forbidden City and the Great Wall.

The claim of diversity is hardly confirmed by the fairly simplistic reference to *two megacities* and *ancient monuments* that compose most outsiders' imagined representation of China.

Although the COVID-19 crisis seems to have put educational mobility on hold for a moment in 2020–2021, more than half a million international students were registered at Chinese institutions of higher education in 2018 (Ministry of Education, 2019), which means that, according to Tsegay et al. (2018: 184), 'China is becoming one of the world's leading destination countries for international students from all

DOI: 10.4324/9781351044554-4

over the world'. Jiani (2016: 564) reminds us rightly however that inter-nationalization of Chinese education is not new since 'dating back to the Sui Dynasty (581–618 AD), China has accepted international students'. Today, research on the students' experiences in the Middle Kingdom has also started to grow both in China and internationally (see Dervin et al., 2017; Tian et al., 2020). Many studies have concentrated on the students' intercultural growth, with a broad focus on 'Chinese culture'. Most studies appear to be ambivalent about it (e.g. Tian & Lowe, 2013; Lumkes et al., 2012). In their 2018 article 'Socio-cultural adjustment experiences of international students in Chinese higher education institutions', Tsegay, Zegergish and Ashraf demonstrate that international students at a top Chinese university failed to develop 'adequate knowledge and experiences of Chinese culture', which they seem to limit to 'Chinese beliefs, traditions and ways of life'. Their article is ambiguous about what *culture* includes and excludes.

Many such studies have often treated host institutions as homogeneous and monolithic, purging them of the potential influences of their local plurality on students' intercultural growth and labelling the local students merely as 'Chinese' – disregarding China's internal diversity. We also note that most of these studies, which claim to describe and explore the 'experiences of international students in China', tend to focus on large urban settings (e.g. Beijing, Shanghai) and top 'internationalized' universities (Ding, 2016; Larbi & Fu, 2017).

Using the concept and approach of superdiversity (Vertovec, 2007), as an essential component of interculturality, this chapter complements current studies on the internationalization of Chinese higher education by focusing on the understudied case of so-called *Ethnic-minority serving institutions* (Xiong, 2020), referred to as Minzu universities here. These universities focus on serving all Chinese ethnic groups and are somewhat equivalent to US tribal colleges and universities (Xiong & Jacob, 2020). In China there are 17 Ethnic Minority Colleges and Universities, where members of the 56 Chinese Minzus live and study together. MUC, a national-level institution located in Beijing, is used here as a case study to examine the position and experiences of international students. MUC has a 'key university status' in China and is transdisciplinary, with around 20,000 students and 1,200 staff. Each year around 400 international students are registered at MUC. Its objective is to build a 'first-class ethnic university in the world'. The main campus of MUC is located in the Zhongguancun High-Technology Industry Base in Beijing, near top universities such as Renmin University of China and Peking University.

On the MUC campus, members of the official 56 Minzu groups of China live and study together in different kinds of programs. International students joining the university can take myriad different degree programs, with many focusing on Minzu issues. For example, at Bachelor's level, on top of public finance and education, they can study Chinese Minority Language and Literature (Korean, Uygur, amongst others) and Minority Music Performance; at Master's level, Chinese Ethnic Minority Economics, History of Chinese Ethnic Minorities and Tibetology; and at PhD level, History of Chinese Ethnic Minorities, Chinese Ethnic Minority Arts and Ethnic Law. Considering the superdiversity that is represented by both the social–interactional and study characteristics of MUC, we hypothesize that such a rich educational context could have a positive influence on international students' intercultural growth, especially in terms of experience, perceptions of China and reflections on Self and Other (Holliday, 2010). Seventeen international students from this superdiverse institution were interviewed to test these hypotheses.

Minzu superdiversity as a special entry into interculturality?

This section frames this study and proposes to use the concept and approach of superdiversity, combined with the notion of Minzu, to explore interculturality as a fluid notion that goes beyond culturalism (culture, especially 'national culture', as an explanation for all) and essentialism (e.g. Dervin, 2016; Holliday, 2010).

Problematizing superdiversity

The concept and approach of superdiversity does not exist in Chinese. There is one word for *pluralism, diversification,* but also *multiculturalism* in the language: 多元化 (duōyuán huà). 多 refers to *many/much, numerous, more, multi-;* 元 to *perspectives, parts* (but also to the Chinese currency unit) and 化 to *transform, change into.* The last character 化 also composes the Chinese word for *culture,* which originally gave it the connotation of *change* (culture as a process of constant change, Fang, 2019). The idea of *diversity* in Chinese thus connotes multiplicity and change at the same time, that is, a complex phenomenon. The term 多元化 appears to be somewhat similar to superdiversity since it indicates the idea of *diversification of diversity.*

Introduced in 2007 as a convoluted analytical lens of the multifaceted (internal and international) migration flows in the British context by Steven Vertovec, superdiversity is used mostly to describe today's link between the demographic complexities of ('Western') postmodern societies and political, economic, policy, technological and socio-cultural changes. Vertovec (2007: 1025) describes superdiversity as the 'transformative diversification of diversity'. According to Arnaut and Spotti (2015: 1):

> Superdiversity rests on the growing awareness that over the past two and a half decades the demographic, sociopolitical, cultural, and sociolinguistic face of societies worldwide has been changing due to ever faster and more mobile communication technologies and software infrastructures, along with the ever-expanding mobility and migration activity related to major geopolitical changes around 1990.

Many research fields use the concept and approach: anthropology, geography, law, linguistics, political science, and urban planning (amongst others). The concept has been used to describe many and varied phenomena such as cultural and linguistic elements in different countries such as Belgium, Egypt, Israel, Italy, Japan, Nigeria and Zimbabwe. Superdiversity is often presented as a critique and an alternative 'way of talking about diversity' beyond, for example, the dichotomy of *multiculturalism* and *interculturalism* (Blommaert & Rampton, 2011; Fomina, 2010). What is more, according to Blommaert (2015: 82), the concept and approach can help scholars move beyond 'the rules of a spatially imagined political, historical, social, cultural and linguistic monocentricity'. Ndhlovu (2015: 33) claims that one of the most important consequences of superdiversity is 'the increase in the lack of predictability of people's identities, their belief systems, their linguistic repertoires and how their needs can best be met both by government and non-government agencies'.

In 2017 Vertovec reevaluated the influence of the concept in global research. He notes that superdiversity is used in many, varied and sometimes problematic ways in research:

- A synonym for 'very much' diversity (Aspinall & Song, 2013);
- A way of talking about the presence of 'more ethnicity' (people from more countries) (Syrett & Lyons, 2007);
- A backdrop for a study, a new condition or setting (Burdsey, 2013);
- A call to move beyond ethnicity and to include additional identity markers such as gender;
- A call for methodological reassessment of studying, e.g. communication and the Structure (Blommaert, 2015);
- A multidimensional reconfiguration of social forms to include multiple variables when analysing diversity (Longhi, 2013);

- A device for drawing attention to new social complexities such as globalization and migration, ethnic categories and social identities, and new social formations.

For Vertovec (2017: 125), the latter, which he refers to as 'the search for better ways to describe and analyse new social patterns, forms and identities arising from migration-driven diversification', is the most appealing aspect of superdiversity. On top of these aspects, Vertovec (2017: 126) asserts that diversification leads to new and/or revised phenomena such as representations (prejudice), inequality and segregation, but also new encounters with space and 'contact' (so-called *cosmopolitanism* and *creolization*). Superdiversity as a concept and an approach is meant to support scholars in moving beyond the essentializing of groups by being critical of methodological nationalism and ethno-national perspectives (Vertovec, 2007).

Many scholars have also assessed the use of superdiversity in research. This is the case of Finex Ndhlovu (2015) in an important article entitled 'A decolonial critique of diaspora identity theories and the notion of diversity'. In the article the scholar reviews the limitations of superdiversity, which we find to be important for our study:

- Although superdiversity tries to describe what is referred to as 'new' phenomena, Ndhlovu (2015: 34) claims that 'there is absolutely nothing new and novel about this since migration is not a new phenomenon at all', reminding us that pre-modern and pre-colonial African societies also experienced 'superdiversity' but have been labelled otherwise by Western-centric research. Mentioning Turner and Khondker's (2010) *Globalization East and West*, he also reminds us that in the Middle Ages mosques were built in China for Arab Muslim traders (Guangzhou and the former capital of Xian).
- Following Makoni (2012), Ndhlovu (2015: 34) is critical of the illusion of equality, social justice and positivity created by superdiversity as referring to changing and multidimensional patterns, as if they were taking place in a neutral and symmetrical world.
- Superdiversity as a Western-centric concept seems to impose a worldview of identities 'often masked behind discourses of universalism, modernity, globalization and other similar terminologies' (Ndhlovu, 2015: 28). Ndhlovu (2015: 29) thus asserts that superdiversity eclipses alternative explanatory and analytical frameworks, especially from the Global South, such as Decoloniality and Southern Theory.

In the field of ICE, Holliday (2010: 74) warns us about the somewhat resistant 'lack of belief that the non-Western Other can be complex and sophisticated just like us'. As such, the international literature on the concept of superdiversity seems to ignore the Chinese context. Very few publications were identified about the topic of superdiversity or superdiversity was used as an approach in research on China. The few available studies focus on some aspects of language issues: for instance, papers have been published on Guangzhou in the South of the country (Liang, 2014) and on the multi-ethnic city Enshi (Dong et al., 2012: 349). Varis and Wang (2011), in their study of the Internet in China, examine both the 'heterogeneity' and the multiple layers of normativity of superdiversity in the Chinese virtual sphere. Some studies of superdiversity relate to Chineseness but in contexts of migration. For instance, Huang (2018) in *Discourses of Chineseness and Superdiversity*, focused on superdiversity and difference in the British Chinese diaspora.

What discussions of superdiversity in relation to study abroad in China, especially within the context of Minzu institutions, could help us achieve and take into account include:

- According to Fanshawe and Sriskandrajah (2010), the potential main benefit of considering superdiversity as a lens is that 'people can't be put in a box anymore', that is, in culturalist boxes (Holliday, 2010). This can also help scholars revise established differences and hierarchies related to discourses of multiculturalism and interculturality (Vertovec, 2017). This is important to move beyond Blommaert's (2015) 'monocentricity' and to take into account the fact that 'people's identities, their belief systems, their linguistic repertoires' are not always predictable (Ndhlovu, 2015).
- Kell (2013) argues that superdiversity, in relation to sociolinguistic issues, can help us add 'layer upon layer of complexity'. This is where the notion of Chinese Minzu could come into play.

Song and Xia (2020: 3) maintain that 'existing studies on international students' intercultural experiences have not paid adequate attention to the potential impact of the socio-economic and cultural diversity within China, or to the diversity with regard to international students' varied accessibility to linguacultural resources'. This chapter aims to contribute to filling in this gap with a case study at a superdiverse Minzu University in Beijing.

Data and data analysis

In what follows, we wish to contribute to 'diversifying' research on study abroad in China, beyond the implicit/explicit monolith, while problematizing the pros and cons of Minzu. We also wish to propose multi-perspectivity and multidirectionality of thinking about this experience of mobility. Superdiversity serves as a lens to examine the experiences of international students at a Chinese Minzu University. Based on interviews with 17 international students we ask the following questions:

- Why did the students choose this specific superdiverse university?
- What is their experience of it? How much does superdiversity seem to influence their experience?
- What is the impact of the university superdiversity on their views of China and the Chinese?

All in all, we are interested in how much superdiversity seems to guide their experiences of a Minzu University.

Seventeen international students were interviewed for this in-depth study of MUC as a superdiverse context for internationalization. We recruited them through purposeful sampling (Patton, 2002). All the countries represented by the students belong to the group of 138 countries of the Belt and Road Initiative (BRI) (also known as the One Belt One Road (一带一路, yi dai yi lu) and the New Silk Road). According to the Green Belt and Road Initiative Centre (https://green-bri.org/belt-and-road-initiative-quick-info), the BRI has represented China's major international cooperation and economic strategy since 2013, focusing on policy coordination, facilities connectivity, unimpeded trade, financial integration and people-to-people bonds. Twelve of the students were from countries bordering China, with some of them sharing linguistic and cultural characteristics with Chinese Minzus (e.g. students 8 and 16). The students in our research were all degree students (Master's level) studying Chinese as a second language at MUC. Apart from an Italian student, all the other students came from different parts of Africa and Asia.

Each interview lasted between 30 and 45 minutes and were led in both Chinese and English. For the sections in Chinese, they were critically and reflexively translated, following the principles of the sinologist Billeter (2014). The analysis was done by means of discourse analysis, in its dialogical form (see e.g. Matusov et al., 2019). Combing through the interviews, using linguistic elements such as represented discourses (i.e. using the voice of others to support a claim), subjectively marked terms (such as adjectives and verbs, see Johansson & Suomela-Salmi, 2011), we have identified specificities and similarities in the way superdiversity seems to have influenced (or not) how the participants describe and problematize their stay in China and their engagement with Minzu superdiversity.

Table 3.1 Information about the students

Student	Nationality	Gender
1	Indonesian	F
2	Indonesian	F
3	South Korean	F
4	Uzbek	M
5	South Korean	M
6	Uzbek	M
7	Lao	M
8	Mongolian	M
9	Egyptian	F
10	Thai	M
11	Vietnamese	F
12	Congolese	F
13	Kazakh	M
14	Uzbek	M
15	Pakistani	M
16	Vietnamese	F
17	Italian	M

Analysis: study abroad experiences in a superdiverse Chinese context

The analytical part consists of three sections. In the first section, we examine the reasons mentioned by the students for choosing China and MUC as study contexts, and try to identify the role of superdiversity in their arguments. The second section focuses on the students' social life in relation to Minzu. Finally, the third section uses the three keywords of superdiversity, identity and interculturality to explore what the students claim to have learned about China, being located in a superdiverse campus.

Reasons for choosing China and Minzu

This first section presents the reasons why the students chose a Minzu University in China. At first when they discuss their general choices for Mainland China, they tend to follow similar paths as students in other studies (Jiani, 2016). Interestingly though, Altbach's (2004) push-pull model for international student mobility, whereby students are pushed by unfavourable conditions in their countries and pulled by opportunities in the other country, was not confirmed. Some of the students were attracted by what could be labelled as Chinese cultural elements (Jiani, 2016). For instance, two students from Indonesia mention their interests in different aspects of Chinese 'culture':

Excerpt 1 – Student 2

I started learning Chinese in high school, and I majored in Chinese as an undergraduate. Since I was young, I have been interested in Chinese. I have watched a lot of TV series and movies about ancient China, and I have been very interested in Chinese scenery and culture.

For this student, the interest in China appears to correspond to canonical knowledge about 'Ancient times', nature and the generic and polysemic idea of 'culture'. Interestingly the other student mentions the fact that a very popular contemporary Chinese singer 周杰伦 (Jay Chou) triggered her interest in China:

Excerpt 2 – Student 1

Five years ago, I went to Singapore and that time I went to a big concert. I didn't know who was singing then, and my friend told me his name is Jay Chou. And I wondered where this Jay Chou came from and at that time, I felt like I should marry him. And then I thought I should learn Chinese and I can marry him. This is the real reason why I should choose China and why I should learn Chinese. So, my first reason is because I like Jay Chou.

Unlike the other student, a somewhat random encounter with a rap artist led to her motivation to get to know China and the Chinese language. In general, we note that the interests of the students in China mostly relate to certain 'typical' – see stereotypical – aspects of Chineseness (see Jiani, 2016).

Some other students refer to their interests in business and economic affairs as motivations for studying in China. As such, one of the Uzbek students mentions the important role of China's economy:

Excerpt 3 – Student 6

When I was young, I was very interested in China. In Uzbekistan, I majored in international economy and China's economy is developing rapidly. My father also worked in China for two years, and my teacher recommended me to come to China to study Chinese for one year and continue my research for four years.

Two voices are used to add to his motivation for choosing China: his father's, who had himself worked in China, and a teacher's. Often, the influence of others on choosing China as a destination is obvious in what the students declare (Jiani, 2016).

In a similar vein, a South Korean student mentions his expectations concerning the role of China in his future career:

Excerpt 4 – Student 5

I majored in economics in college, and the school offered Chinese courses, so I studied Chinese for six months. I'm interested in Chinese, and I hope to have something to do with it in my future job, so I want to know about the situation, life, courses and culture of China. China in my imagination is different from reality. For example, time passes quickly in China, so I need to pay attention to time management.

Like many other students in our research, Student 5 notes that he also wishes to confront his own perceptions of China with the reality. Interestingly, like three other students, he uses the word 'imagination' to discuss his pre-conceived ideas about the Middle Kingdom ('China in my imagination is different from reality'). This could indicate an opening towards Chinese superdiversity, maybe, beyond the monolith.

In what follows we turn to how the students justify their application for programmes at MUC. Here again there appear to be distinctive patterns. Several students mentioned the recommendations they had received from friends and teachers for choosing MUC:

Excerpt 5 – Student 11

I'm here because someone introduced me to MUC. He's a student here.

Excerpt 6 – Student 12

I was introduced by a friend. Through him, I met someone in Congo who told me that the education of MUC was very good, and I believed it.

Excerpt 7 – Student 16

It was fate, because there was one of my senior students who studied in the school, and then she was very good in the school, and then she recommended it to me . . . and then I asked my teacher to help me apply, and came here.

These three students, two from Vietnam and one from Congo, have all met someone who was a former student or a current student at MUC from their own countries and then decided to apply. The argument that their contact is said to have used is that of the good quality of the institution ('very good').

For two students, the choice of MUC relates (in)directly to exchange programmes between their home universities and MUC. Student 17, from Italy, was first an exchange student at MUC before joining the institution as a degree student:

Excerpt 8 – Student 17

Actually, for the first time I went to Minzu because I was studying in [a city in Southern Italy], it is one of the first schools in Europe where you can study Chinese. It is a very old school, it is very important. And my university has cooperation with Minzu University. But it is not for Chinese language, it is for Tibetan language. In my school, you can study Tibetan too. But now there are not a lot of students who study the Tibetan language, so they give me the possibility to study Chinese here.

Through a scholarship meant for those majoring in Tibetan from his Italian university, Student 17 was first able to continue his studies in the Chinese language. One could say that Chinese Minzu superdiversity allowed him indirectly to study in China. Student 1, from Indonesia, had the opportunity to do an exchange at a top university in Beijing (Renmin University) through her home university but chose MUC instead for the following reasons:

Excerpt 9 – Student 1

I should go to Beijing, my university cooperates with another university, that is, I should choose Renmin University. However, I think I should meet more Chinese people, but not only Han majority, I can meet more ethnic minority people here. And firstly, in the rankings, Minzu University is also a good university in China, and even in Beijing. Secondly, I want to read more about China's minority.

Chinese superdiversity seems to have been decisive for Student 1. For her, Renmin University in Beijing would have meant spending time with 'Han majority' students, while MUC offered opportunities to develop relations with superdiverse individuals.

In general, the students mention their awareness of the fact that MUC is a good university but not as prestigious as other universities such as Peking University or Renmin University. However, like Student 1, the superdiverse profile of the institution seems to have won over. Student 7 from Laos claims that he knew nothing about MUC and checked its profile on the Internet:

Excerpt 10 – Student 7

I didn't have any image or information about Chinese universities. So, I checked the Internet. MUC came out. MUC is very close to the Chinese People's University [i.e. Renmin University]. I learned something about it and I thought it was very interesting. There are many ethnic minorities in China, and I would like to know more about them. For foreigners, they only know the Han Minzu. Here, I think some Minzus are very similar to mine. For example, my master's supervisor is Bouyei, and when I learn Bouyei, I feel it is very similar to the language of our nation.

Interestingly, Student 7 notes a similarity between his own language group (Laotian speakers) and the Bouyei language spoken by some Chinese Minzus in the southern Guizhou Province of China. Laotian and Bouyei are both Kra-Dai languages, tonal languages spoken in Southeast Asia, South China and Northeast India with around 93 million speakers. The student refers to the imagined voice of the figure of the 'foreigner' in the excerpt – in opposition to his own interest in Minzu superdiversity – to make them say that they don't know much Minzus.

In Excerpt 11, the student from Egypt shares the questions she asked her teacher before choosing MUC. The superdiverse argument is found in the teacher's answers ('he said . . .'):

Excerpt 11 – Student 9

Before I came here, I asked our teacher 'Which university is the best?' He said this university was good for us. There are many ethnic groups in this university, and there are many Chinese ethnic groups here. Before we come, we will ask a few questions: 'What are the grades of this university?' We are newcomers and the application for Minzu University is very welcoming to us. And there are not so many Egyptians here, like me. So, I will have more opportunities to be with the Chinese, and if there are a lot of Egyptians, I will be with the Egyptians.

One extra argument, on top of the benefits of getting to know Chinese superdiversity, is about the low number of students from her own country at MUC. In the most research on study abroad in China and other parts of the world, the presence of co-nationals is often seen as counterproductive in terms of adaptation, language use and learning and intercultural awareness since students are said to be spending too much time with each other (e.g. Pho & Schartner, 2019). As a student specializing in Chinese language and culture at MUC, opportunities to meet and speak with Chinese speakers are often seen as primordial (Gong et al., 2020).

In this first analytical section, we note that most students chose MUC because of an acquaintance or information they found on the Internet. Although it is a good – but not prestigious - Chinese university, most of them refer to the benefits of Minzu superdiversity as a reason for choosing MUC as their destination. Although the students do not go into detail as to what this means concretely – apart from 'getting to know China' beyond a somewhat imagined 'Han' image – the student from Laos – a country which shares a 475-km border with China – does make a clear reference to the linguistic similarities between Laotian and Bouyei, one of the Chinese Minzu languages. This could be a sign that the generic 'boxes' of China and the Chinese are expanded by the student and open up to superdiversity (Ndhlovu, 2015).

A superdiverse social life?

In this section, we examine how much of an impact a superdiverse institution like MUC might have on the students' social lives. First, we note that Chinese, English and first languages are used to communicate with others, based on individual skills and shared languages. Second, the interviews reveal that the students' social lives are represented by interactions with people referred to as 'friends' who seem to be composed of groups of international students from MUC or other universities in Beijing and/or 'Chinese students', who appear to be Han students in most cases. As we shall see, references to Minzus are rare when the students discuss their social lives. There could be different reasons why: 1 The students lump them all together under the label 'Chinese people/students'; 2 Minzu aspects are not so relevant to them since they study Chinese and feel the pressure to use the language; 3 There is a lack of access to Minzu students other than Han students.

But, in general, we get the impression that there are very few opportunities to interact with Chinese students. This seems to relate to minimum joint activities organized by the university, but also to international students flocking together (see similar results in Hussain & Hong, 2019). For Student 16: 'Han students and foreign students feel that they can't be in touch with each other because they are cut off'. Again, the fact that Han students are systematically mentioned – rather than other Minzu students – might derive from the fact that the students specialize in Chinese and feel the need to practice this particular language.

For some students, their social lives seem divided between socializing with Chinese and international friends – depending on contexts. As such, Student 1 clearly dichotomizes these encounters:

Excerpt 12 – Student 1

I have class with all of my friends, Chinese friends actually. And after I have finished my class, I always spend time playing with my foreign friends. Maybe for study I will be with my Chinese friends. It will be more helpful and we will help each other. But after class, Chinese people, you know, they really, really like to study hard. But I want to have a balanced life: I should study hard but I will also be playing harder than I study. So, after I finish my class I will be with my foreign friends, because we can speak English. It will make me feel freer. Yeah, because every day we should speak Chinese. It's like after I wake up I should speak Chinese and then I want to sleep. I should speak Chinese. It really makes me so dizzy.

The compartmentalization of daily social encounters presented by Student 1 (and shared by many other students) appears to be utilitarian: time spent with the (generic) Chinese is used for studying, while time with international ('foreign') students is for 'playing'. Several explanations are offered by the student: spending time with international students means using English and thus relaxing, while the use of Chinese makes her feel 'dizzy' and pressured. She also uses the typical representation of 'Chinese people (. . .) like to study hard', which is presented as a barrier to socialization after class (see the same argument provided by students at an elite university in Beijing in Dervin, Härkönen, Yuan, Chen, & Zhang, 2020). Student 4 from Uzbekistan told us that, at the time of the interview, they were preparing for exams and that he did not get to meet his Chinese friends since they were not in class together anymore.

A minority of the students that we interviewed (one from Korea, Student 5, another from Congo, Student 12) admit spending most of their time with co-nationals.

Excerpt 13 – Student 5

I usually go out with my classmates after class. We often go to Wudaokou because there are a lot of Korean restaurants and products there. Because there are a lot of Koreans in China, we spend time together.

Wudaokou (五道口), an area in Beijing close to MUC and popular amongst students at top surrounding universities such as Peking University, is often referred to as Korea-town (Kim, 2010). Korean students and entrepreneurs but also Chinese Korean Minzu people hang around in the area. The Congolese student also admits socializing with her co-nationals, while spending time at home and being in contact with her Chinese and foreign friends online:

Excerpt 14 – Student 12

I usually don't go out. I like to stay at home. I like to watch Chinese TV shows and movies. I'm going out with my compatriots. I have a Chinese friend and a foreign friend. But we basically don't see each other. Everyone is very busy and is in their own place. I'm in my own place, too. I don't want to bother them either. I basically don't go out with the Chinese, but more of my friends, we often exchange on WeChat. We help each other.

The repetition of the verb 'to go out' structures the student's excerpt: first she claims that she 'does not usually go out', then she refers to going out with her 'compatriots' and, third, the verb is used to exclude the 'Chinese' ('I basically don't go out with the Chinese'). Compartmentalization of social interaction is taking place here too.

The Lao student discusses her social interaction, not in terms of nationality, but of co-languaging.

Excerpt 15 – Student 7

Interviewer: So who are your friends here?
Student 7: Thai friends.
Interviewer: And you speak Chinese together, or English?
Student 7: We speak Laotian . . . it's the same language.

Laotian, which is of the same language family as Thai, is inter-intelligible and thus creates opportunities for communication with Thai students, Student 7's 'friends'. In the next excerpt, which follows the previous one, the interviewer asks the student if her language has some similarities to some Minzu languages spoken in Yunnan Province in southwestern China:

Excerpt 16 – Student 7

Interviewer: Do some ethnic minorities in Yunnan have the same language as yours?

Student 7: I'm not in touch with them, but there's a language called Zhuang. Zhuang and our language are a bit the same, but not a lot. For everyday communication, we can understand each other. But the professional vocabulary of the modern academic field is not the same.

Although there could be an opportunity for interacting in a common language, Student 7 does not seem to have reaped the benefit of this similarity with some of China's superdiversity to engage with them.

Only one student, amongst the ones we interviewed, seemed to have a big interest in Minzus. In what follows, the Italian student describes his social interactions. After talking about the room that he shares with an Irish male student – 'I don't have any problem with him, because the culture is not different', Student 17 explains:

Excerpt 17 – Student 17

Student 17: I don't have a lot of Han friends. I have a lot of Tibetan friends. A lot of Xinjiang friends. That is why I love Minzu. That is a really good point of this university. You can understand others. All kinds of people who are not Han. China is not Beijing or Shanghai, it is a lot of other places. I love these places, so that is why I chose to come here, because I can understand Tibetan of China. I am a fan of Tibet. All the culture, all the history, I really like it. When I come here, wow . . . a lot of Tibetan people, I can talk with them.
Interviewer: How did you meet them?
Student 17: In school it is very easy to meet them. If you bring a football, you can find them. If you go jogging, say hello . . . Before I didn't like this, for I was always with foreigners, a French guy, an Irish guy, always together. Now it is different. Because I am living everyday with language course students, they are coming and going, travelling, they are here just for four months. But the minority students are always here.

As a reminder, this student studied twice at MUC: first as an exchange student, followed by a stay as a degree student. During his first stay, he admits spending most of his time with other international students, but, since he started his degree at MUC he has been able to spend more time with 'minority [Minzu] students'. What this excerpt from the interview shows is that Student 17 is eager to meet Minzu students, especially from Tibet since he is 'a fan of Tibet'. For the student, the message that his time at Minzu seems to have triggered is that China is not homogeneous (he mentions Beijing, Shanghai and Han people) but superdiverse, through the (snapshot) example of Tibet. When asked directly what his time at MUC did to him in terms of perceiving China, he claims:

Excerpt 18 – Student 17

It changed. Now I can understand more compared to my classmates before. They are studying in Italy, in my university, but they don't know what real China is. So that is so important. I changed my view about China. It is a great experience for me in Minzu. Maybe those who study in Renmin, it is like going to America. A lot of foreign students, they are the same. But here, you have to face the real China.

What Student 17 seems to explain here is that MUC differs from other Chinese universities, giving the example of a top university like Renmin University. For the student, being an international student at Renmin is like 'going to America', in other words, the student seems to assert that this university does not create a real sense of *dépaysement*, an English word from the French for the feeling of not being at home, in a foreign or different place, a change of scenery. On the contrary, what MUC seems to be doing to students like him is to allow them to 'face the real China'. We note that the phrase 'real China' is used twice in this excerpt. Based on what Student 7 affirms about Minzu, this phrase could refer to Chinese 'superdiversity'.

Finally, when asked about his travels in China, Student 17 shows that his interest and curiosity about Chinese superdiversity have guided his destination decisions:

Excerpt 19 – Student 17

I was in lots of places in China. Not a lot, cause China is huge. But I have a lot of experience with my friend's family. That was great! I was in my friend's house, because he is a Tujiazu. He said, during Chinese New Year, 'You are here, you are alone, you should come to my house.' I really had such a great time. We went to a lot of places, that was beautiful. I fell in love with China. And I feel 'Oh China is amazing'. Because Beijing, I mean, is just a city. But China is all except this big city. Not Shenzhen, not Shanghai.

Student 17 is the only one who mentions spending time with a Minzu family outside the campus, and outside Beijing. The excerpt is composed of positive evaluative discourses ('That was great!'; 'I really had such a great time'; 'That was beautiful'; 'Oh China is amazing'). Recounting his visit to a friend's family, who was a Tuija, a member of China's eighth largest Minzu in the Wuling Mountains (population of over 8 million), the student describes Chinese superdiversity as different from megacities such as Beijing but also Shanghai and Shenzhen, which he evaluates as 'just cit[ies]'.

In this section, we have seen that superdiverse MUC does not seem to lead to systematic social interactions with a diversified community. Students seem to be spending time in compartmentalized groups (international, co-national and Chinese), with very little space and/or opportunities for interacting with different Minzus. Student 17 from Italy appears to be an exception, especially in his references to Tibetan and Tuija Minzus. Although the students were eager to join MUC for its superdiversity at first, when they discuss their social lives, this aspect seems minor.

Learning about Chinese superdiversity: identity and interculturality

Although interaction with Minzu superdiversity appears to be limited in the students' interviews, this section examines if and what the international students seem to have gained in terms of knowledge about Chinese superdiversity. What we notice is that reflecting on Minzu superdiversity leads students to ponder over identity and interculturality – and in many cases cross-border identities.

Some students admit not being aware of Chinese superdiversity before coming to the Middle Kingdom. This is the case of the student from Pakistan, who explains how he has learned about Minzus during lectures at MUC:

Excerpt 20 – Student 15

To be honest, in coming to China I did not know it was a country with many ethnic groups. I thought it was only the Han nationality. So, when I first came, I found that there were 56 ethnic groups. I was surprised. There are some literary and cultural lessons in our class and then the teachers often introduce us to all Minzus and their specific culture, so I now learn and understand more.

The use of the phrase 'the specific culture' might hint at a limited and culturalist approach to Minzu superdiversity. Student 16 from Vietnam seemed to know more about Chinese superdiversity, especially in relation to cross-border Minzu groups with similar language backgrounds. In the following excerpt, however, the student contrasts the knowledge she thought she had before and during her stay:

Excerpt 21 – Student 16

I knew a little before coming to China. I know that there are 56 ethnic groups in China, and some ethnic groups are somewhat similar to us, such as Dai and Jing ethnic groups. Before I came to China, I felt that the language and appearance of the Chinese ethnic minorities were different from those of the Han nationality, and some of their customs were also different. I thought that they were usually on the mountains and seldom came down to the plains. Then when I came to China, I found that it was not completely the case. There were some differences in customs and habits. Every ethnic minority has its own customs and habits. However, their appearance is sometimes not very different from that of the Han nationality.

In the excerpt the student refers to the Dai and Jing Minzus in southeastern China, which she assumed were very different from the Han majority – maybe in terms of economic development, see the comment on them living in the mountains in the excerpt. What the sojourn seems to have contributed for Student 16 is an awareness of the continuum of difference-similarity in terms of Chinese Minzu superdiversity (Han + Dai and Jing), thus 'thinking beyond the box' of differentialism and essentialism (Dervin, 2016).

Student 3 from South Korea makes the same comment concerning facial features and physical traits twice (Liu & Dervin, 2020). For her, it was surprising that many Chinese from different Minzus did not look 'Chinese':

Excerpt 22 – Student 3

Before I came to China, I only knew that there were 56 nationalities in China. But after I came here, I found many people who don't look like Chinese. They may be ethnic minorities like Russian, Kazakh, Uygur, etc., but they are all Chinese, which surprised me a lot.

I now know more about different parts of China. I think some people, such as Kazakhs, Uyghurs, they look like Westerners, but in fact they are Chinese, which is amazing.

In this excerpt the student is made to question her representations of the way Chinese people look – their facial features and physical traits. She notes on two occasions during the interview that some Minzus (Chinese Kazakhs, Russians and Uyghurs) look different and even label them as 'look[ing] like Westerners' – a misidentification reported by some Chinese themselves (e.g. Wu, 1991: 170).

This urges another South Korean to ask the Minzu students he meets on campus their Minzu affiliation as stated in the following excerpt:

Excerpt 23 – Student 5

In class, if I think someone's appearance is different from other people's, I will ask him what ethnic minority he is. When I was a freshman in college, I studied Chinese and ethnic minorities, but there are no pictures in the textbook. I only know that there are many ethnic minorities, but I don't know their specific characteristics. But after coming here, I can distinguish some of the minorities.

This leads him to assert having learned to tell the Minzu of some of the people he meets.

Another interesting phenomenon for some of the international students is the proximity between some Minzus and their own peoples in terms of culture and language. One can assert that Chinese superdiversity thus makes them reflect on their own identity and interculturality in terms of similarity and difference. Student 7 from Laos comments on clothing from some Minzus which were reminiscent of his own:

Excerpt 24 – Student 7

I went to the Museum of Nationalities and saw clothes from the Bai and Zhuang ethnic groups. It reminded me of the ones we have, and we feel very proud. We also want to show it to our Chinese friends. We also have these kind of clothes. Then, I think Chinese ethnic minorities also have their own clothes, but they don't wear them very much. They wear them only on important festivals. But in Laos, we all wear our own national clothes at school or at work.

In this excerpt the student notes similarities between Laotian clothing and Bai and Zhuang Minzu groups (respectively located in southwest China and the Guangxi Zhuang Autonomous Region in southern China), which she evaluates positively, using a generic 'we', probably referring to her own ethnic group back in Laos ('we feel very proud'). At the end of the excerpt, however, she contrasts usage of the clothes in the two countries. A Vietnamese student also comments on these similarities (Student 11) of clothing between Vietnamese and Jing people from southeastern China. This student, like others, wished that MUC organized more joint activities with Minzu students in order to explore such similarities.

Finally, since many of the participants are from border countries, they are often mistaken for being Chinese themselves. Their different accents, facial features and physical traits lead to them being mislabelled. For example, Student 16 from Vietnam explains that many Chinese people think that her accent in Chinese is from the South but they assume, based on her face, that she is from the Xinjiang Uyghur Autonomous Region, bordering Afghanistan, India, Kazakhstan, Kyrgyzstan, Mongolia, Pakistan and Tajikistan, where many Turkic peoples live. The Xinjiang mislabelling was also mentioned by Student 10 from Thailand. Student 11 also from Vietnam explains when asked if she is mistaken for a Minzu student:

Excerpt 25 – Student 11

They don't know what race I am. They only say that I am a minority from Guangxi, or then Yunnan, and then I also say that I am a minority, because I am a Jing race. The Jing race is the dominant race in our country, but it is a minority in your China and more in Guangxi.

The guessing game from the Chinese concerning her identity makes her explain the fact that she shares an identity with some Minzu Chinese (cross-border identity), that of Jing. She also explains that, unlike China, her 'Minzu' (which she refers to as 'race' in English) in Vietnam is the majority on the other side of the border.

In general, the attitude of the 'Chinese' is presented as very positive towards foreigners. Student 5 from South Korea explains:

Excerpt 26 – Student 5

Once on a train, some Chinese started speaking to me and thought that I was Chinese and offered to say hello to me. Then I said I was a foreigner. 'Oh do you want some apples? Do you eat pears?'

However, Student 6 from Uzbekistan told us of a negative experience based on misidentification:

Excerpt 27 – Student 6

I once lived in a dorm, he thought I was from Xinjiang, the attitude is very bad. I told him I was a foreigner, but he didn't believe me. I showed him my passport. And then he said: 'I'm sorry. I have water. Would you like to drink it?'

Replaying a dialogue with a dormmate, the student shows how the misidentification of a person from Xinjiang led to mistreatment, which was the corrected by revealing the truth about his national identity. The direct quote from the dormmate shows a shift in his attitude once the misidentification was 'corrected'.

This section has demonstrated that although relations with Minzu peoples appear limited on a daily basis, in general the students have learned a lot about Chinese Minzu superdiversity. For students from cross-border countries, because of their facial features, physical traits and accents in Mandarin Chinese, they can be misidentified, which seems to make them reflect on identity, interculturality and superdiversity.

[Pause]

This chapter proposed to complement current studies on internationalization of Chinese higher education, focusing on 17 international students from different Belt and Road countries. The context of the study was an original one which has not been, to our knowledge, the focus of research on study abroad in China: a superdiverse Minzu University located in Beijing, where members of the 56 Chinese Minzus live and study together. Most studies on international students in China – but also in other contexts – have treated local universities as somewhat homogeneous and monolithic, purging them of their potential superdiversity. In the case of China, most studies have also looked into top elite universities in megacities such as Beijing and Shanghai.

Three sets of questions were asked in this study. Although the university is not deemed prestigious compared to top universities in Beijing, we discovered that superdiversity was reported as a pull factor for most students. However, their experience of Minzu superdiversity appeared to be limited to linguistic and cultural snapshots of it in most cases. This might give the impression that it serves as a mere slogan in the students' narratives. As such, only one student seemed to have made a conscious effort to link up with members of diverse Minzus. We note that the students' knowledge and awareness of the important aspect of Minzu in Chineseness appeared strong when they discussed what they had learned from the university. They also seemed to have modified many of their representations of China as a place of imagined monocentricity (Blommaert, 2015) where everybody looks the same and speaks the same language.

Probably the most fascinating aspect of our study is the identification issues relating to cross-border identities. Students whose facial features, physical traits and accents in Mandarin Chinese make them 'look' and 'sound' Chinese, or, like members of Chinese Minzus, have to face situations of misidentification which are unique to them. Through these misidentifications, they become themselves part of superdiversity, in the sense given to it by Ndhlovu (2015): their perceived identities lead to a lack of predictability for those they meet. There is a need to explore these elements in further studies since they can have an influence on study abroad experiences interculturally.

In terms of combining Minzu and superdiversity, we discovered that the way the students discuss Minzu appears to be synonymous with 'very much' Chinese diversity and the presence of 'more ethnicity' (Vertovec, 2017). Discussions of Minzu also demonstrate that its superdiverse characteristics allow them to think of China beyond 'the box' (Fanshawe & Sriskandrajah, 2010). In some rare cases, especially because of the mis-identification that they experienced, Minzu as superdiversity allowed the students to note some negative aspects such as discrimination and/or inequality (Vertovec, 2017).

It is important to note that our study was limited by the choice of students who specialized in Chinese language and culture, which seemed to have an influence on their interests in exploring Minzu superdiversity.

Our study has some repercussions for both scholars and ethnic-serving minority institutions like MUC.

First, it is important for research on study abroad to expand its vision of 'locality' to correspond to the idea of superdiversity, which cannot but affect (positively but also negatively) any educational context today. Putting an end to treating 'locals' homogeneously should be a priority.

Second, international students should have the opportunity to both reflect critically on locality through the lens of superdiversity in, for example, courses on interculturality, which would not train them to learn about the confusing and somewhat essentializing idea of the 'local culture' – as is often the case (see Dervin, 2016) – but to gain knowledge and analytical tools to open up their mind to the omnipresence of superdiversity. What is more, the students should be given opportunities to meet and discuss these issues with as many different 'local' people as possible, avoiding too much compartmentalization of social interactions, so they can apply this knowledge to practice. As such, a context like MUC represents an ideal laboratory for such work. While they reflect on Chinese superdiversity, international students should also be equipped to transfer these reflexive skills to their own context. According to Abdallah-Pretceille (2004), seeing (super)diversity in Self can also help see and accept superdiversity in the 'Other'.

Third, cross-border *mélange* and mixing were very clear in some of the students' discourses. Although national borders matter and are symbolic of important identities, it would be important for international students – but also students in general – to reflect on the geographical, historical, linguistic and cultural aspects of these phenomena to facilitate encounters and stimulate curiosity towards the 'Other'. For instance, the Lao student who made friends with some Thai students, using a language they shared in common, did not seem so eager to link up with, for example, Zhuang students from the other side of the border, in China, who also speak their language. Such superdiverse encounters could make internationalization more intercultural and plurilingual.

Finally, for the 'locals', there also appears to be a necessity to learn to question assumptions about facial features, physical traits and identities in order to open up to superdiversity of the 'Other' too and avoid misjudging – and at times 'mistreating' – them.

[Time to reflect]

- Have you ever come across the concept of *superdiversity*? How would you translate it in the languages that you know? How has it been used in research in your own context?

- What difference does a Minzu context seem to make for international students in terms of interculturality? What can be learned from the experiences of the research participants about the benefits and failures of study abroad?

- Were you aware of the complexity of cross-border identities in China? What did you learn about it, reading through the first three chapters of this book?

- How do you understand this statement from one of the participants: 'Studying at Renmin [a top Chinese university in Beijing] is like studying in the US'? What does the student mean? Does it make sense to you?

- If you have travelled abroad, or spent time studying in another country, how many ethnic minority individuals have you met? Did getting to know them allow you to change your perspective on the host country?

- Are there institutions like MUC in your context? If yes, try to find out how popular they are amongst international students and the reasons why they choose them as their destination.

- How could we make sure that we meet as many 'diverse' locals as possible, who can give us a sense of 'local' diversity?

- Have you ever been 'misidentified' in intercultural contexts because of the way you look and/or sound? How did you feel? Were you able to renegotiate your identity with those who misidentified you?

4 Being 'good' at interculturality

Answers from Minzu education

In this chapter, using interculturality as a central and multi-ideological notion for dealing with diversity in education, we examine a group of students' discourses on the notion within the context of Minzu higher education (MUC). In a course on Minzu and interculturality in education, the students were asked to reflect critically and reflexively on the meaning of 'being good at interculturality'. Based on essays that they have written about this issue our chapter provides some answers to the following questions:

- How do the students construct their answers to the issue of 'being good at interculturality'?
- What words do they use in English to formulate their answers? What ideologies seem to be contained in their arguments?
- Because our study is taking place within the specific context of Minzu higher education, how much of this specific context of interculturality seems to influence the students in the way they see 'being good at interculturality'?

Interculturality as a complex figure in a carpet

In Henry James's 1896 novella, *The Figure in the Carpet*, the narrator prides himself in having discovered the true meaning of an author's book in a review that he had just published. However, he overhears the author commenting negatively on his review at a party, arguing that nobody has been able to identify the idea present in all his novels, which he compares to the complex woven figure in a Persian carpet. In the rest of the novella, in vain, the narrator tries to find this secret. To us, interculturality is like the writer's key idea that the novella's narrator wishes to identify. When we think we have put our finger on it, its meaning(s) and connotation(s) disappear in front of our eyes, especially when we are confronted with

DOI: 10.4324/9781351044554-5

the 'Other'. Interculturality is like a complex figure in a carpet, a multidimensional space of encounters between different policies, practices, philosophies and economic-political ideologies. However, it is rarely dealt with in such complex ways.

Since we use the notion in our work with Minzu students as a central term to discuss issues of diversity within the Chinese context and beyond, what follows serves as a way of problematizing it. It is important to reiterate first that the notion is kaleidoscopic and polyvalent. It means either too much or too little. As hinted at several times in this book, we are somewhat seduced by the complexity of the notion, which is indicated by both its prefix *inter-* and suffix *-ality*, implying (never-ending) processes, relations, co-constructions. Used in different socio-political contexts, a smörgåsbord of perspectives on interculturality is available around the world. Sometimes it is even confused and mixed with other terms such as *multicultural, transcultural* and even *global* (as in *global competence*), meaning the same or something different, and having the same or different politico-economic connotations. We note, however, that some specific Western-centric ideologies seem to dominate the way the world thinks about interculturality, especially in education. In this chapter we understand *ideology* as follows:

> 'Ideology' means strictly a system of ideas elaborated in the light of certain conceptions of what 'ought to be.' It designates a theory of social life which approaches the facts from the point of view of an ideal, and interprets them, consciously or unconsciously, to prove the correctness of its analysis and to justify that ideal. The starting-point is essentially extra-scientific-the ideal. Thus every ideological construction involves the projection of a certain ideal into the future, into the evaluation of the present, and into the past.
>
> (Roucek, 1944: 479)

As a societal project that is coloured by the political, philosophic-social arguments, power relations (e.g. host-guest) and corporate supremacy, interculturality cannot but be discussed, constructed, taught and researched within the realm of ideologies, of the 'ought to be' (versus the 'ought not'). Research and teaching about interculturality are systematically influenced by assumptions in, for example, the words used to deal with the notion ('tolerance', 'democracy'), its premises are taken for granted (as in the order: 'contact with the different "Other" opens our mind') and become the 'truth' with the 'right values'. These often hide behind illusions of *scientificity*. In global education it is important to bear in mind that dominating ideologies tend to be promoted by Western scholars who have some symbolic power such as prestigious institutional affiliations (US/UK universities), publications in top international journals, editorships of book series with top publishers. What is more, these ideologies are passed onto people through different Euro-/Americano-centric ideological Apparatuses such as the Council of Europe, the European Union and the Organisation for Economic Co-operation and Development (OECD), which 'dictate' the way interculturality should be defined, practiced and evaluated (see introduction to this book). Locally, ideologies of interculturality may also have a specific 'flavour' influenced by decision-making and governance: France is famous for its politically driven ideology of *laïcité* (translated poorly in English as 'secularism') which is omnipresent in intercultural education (see e.g. Abdallah-Pretceille, 2004). When *laïcité* is combined with ideologies from, for example, an ideological Apparatus like the OECD or with those of a British scholar of language and intercultural education, the end result might be very contradictory, confusing and even 'unfair' for some scholars, teachers and students alike.

In the context of MUC, bearing in mind the multiplicity of discourses about diversity in the ways Minzu students think about interculturality (see Yuan et al., 2020), we have negotiated and taken three steps to make sure that the students have the possibility to use interculturality as a critical and reflexive tool to deal with issues of diversity. During the lectures the students are trained to unthink and rethink what they claim about diversity and interculturality – and what scholars, educators and decision-makers make of these notions too. Figure 4.1 presents the three steps.

These three steps go hand in hand and entail consistent discussions of the use of terms in Chinese and English to refer to intercultural

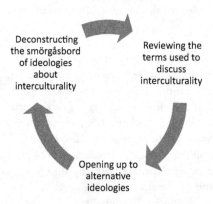

Figure 4.1 The three steps in using interculturality as a critical and reflexive tool

'realities'; noticing how the way one thinks about interculturality and diversity is influenced by many (and often contradictory) ideologies; opening up to alternative ideologies. The steps are described in more details below.

Deconstructing the smörgåsbord of ideologies about interculturality:

- Identifying the sources of global dominating ideologies, supported by global systems of politico-economic institutions;
- Identifying their orders, imposed (inter-)subjectivities and ideological intimidation: what they tell us to believe in; 'ought tos'.

Reviewing the terms used to discuss interculturality:

- Multilingual and 'archaeological' analyses of concepts and notions used in Chinese and English (etymology);
- Critical translation of words (e.g. *tolerance* in Chinese and English, which can have different meanings and connotations).

Opening up to alternative ideologies:

- Identifying alternative ideologies which are localized/silenced in global research/educational worlds;
- Looking at intercultural issues from multiple perspectives, and, possibly, have more opportunities for (re-)negotiation and choices;
- Reimagining interculturality while being aware of re-ideologization.

In what follows, we provide some examples of how we educate the students to systematize their application of the steps. For the step of deconstructing the smörgåsbord of ideologies about interculturality, we review with the students what they (think they) know about learning/teaching objectives of interculturality – what they think one should do to become 'intercultural'. Two points continually emerge amongst the students: interculturality is about 'cultures meeting and/or clashing' and 'stereotypes should be eradicated'. We review these assertions with the students to make them aware of the ideological beliefs hiding behind them. For 'cultures meeting and/or clashing', we explore the history and archaeology of the concept of *culture* and how it has been an overused and abused episteme since the 18th century to create hierarchies between different cultures, even and especially in research ('more civilized', 'politer', 'more punctual', 'more hardworking', 'quieter', see Chemla & Keller, 2017). The step of reviewing the terms in discussions of interculturality is used here too. Fang's aforementioned (2019) book, *Modern Notions of Culture and Civilisation in China*, is introduced to examine how the words *culture* and *civilization* have come to mean what they mean in China today. Fang explains that the two concepts of 文化 *wenhua* (culture) and 文明 *wenming* (civilization) are not stable in China today (Fang, 2019: 113), although their current meanings are borrowed from the West. Fang also shows that when we start surveying the historical use of the two words, we realize that the words 文化 (culture) and 文明 (civilization) have foreign origins in their meanings and connotations, although they have been identified in classic Chinese but with different meanings from today. The semantic changes occurred in the second half of the 19th century, influenced by the 'West', but imported via Japan (Fang, 2019: 62). While 文 (wen) in classic Chinese used to refer to component elements being mixed together (Fang, 2019: 10), 化 (hua) originally indicated *change, formation* or *making*. 文 + 化 used to refer to a situation wherein a change takes place for one side or both sides concerned, as a result of their contact with each other (Fang, 2019: 9). Before it took on its 'Western' meaning, 文明 used to refer to a progressive state of being, thriving development of culture and education (Fang, 2019: 2). Since the two words are somewhat ambiguous in Chinese today, the students learn that they should never assume, when they speak to foreigners in English, that they refer to the same realities when we say *culture* and *civilization*.

The ideas of 'cultural difference', 'knowledge about other cultures', 'culture shock', 'the clash of cultures' are also problematized. The students explore how these could potentially serve as caricatures and simplifications. In order for them to become aware of the instability of the use of these concepts around the world, we show them how the concept of culture can be used as a mere substitute for other concepts in some contexts (Eriksen, 2001). For instance, in some European countries, the concept of *race* cannot be 'voiced', instead decision-makers, scholars and educators might refer to *ethnicity* and/or *culture*, while promoting anti-racism. As far as stereotyping is concerned, the idea that the awareness and knowledge of other cultures can help either reduce or remove stereotypes is strong amongst the students. We spend time deepening their critical and reflexive engagement with the concept by making them aware of the fact that stereotypes are unstable elements that can re-emerge at any moment even when they have been 'suppressed' or that they can easily be substituted by another stereotype.

As a way of summarizing the unthinking and rethinking of both culture and stereotypes – as components of dominating ideologies – the students are made to reflect with us on the types of questions that are asked in intercultural encounters. For instance, the questions 'Where are you from?' (and for some people, the systematic follow-up question, 'Where are you *really* from?'), 'What is your culture?', 'What is your mother tongue?', are all based on the modern ideologies of the nation-state, national identity and national language, and can easily lead to hierarchies rather than encounters. Since the students are from Minzu contexts, they know that answering these questions (for example when meeting a foreigner) often requires making choices in terms of what to answer. Depending on the interlocutor, and the context of interaction, this might lead them to have to make choices between various identities or even to refrain from telling the 'truth' about their origins for fear of discrimination and/or stereotyping. The step of opening up to alternative ideologies is then explored with the students, whereby new ways of thinking about perhaps what to ask when meeting someone for the first time are envisaged.

Bearing in mind the specific context of our study, we have written earlier about the extra complexities in the different layers of discourses, ideologies and multilingual aspects of discussing interculturality, as experienced by Minzu students (Yuan et al., 2020). Through these three steps the students are supported in building up awareness of their own intercultural ecosystem, where complex discourses are enmeshed: so-called 'Western' ideologies (*tolerance, respect, open-mindedness*) with references to American and British scholars such as Byram and Deardorff, but also, and most importantly, MUC's ideological position towards intercultural dialogue (e.g. 'Knowledge corresponds with actions'; 'Diversity in Unity'), Chinese political discourses about Minzus ('Harmony without uniformity'), as well as more localized Minzu discourses ('We Hui[1] learn the language of others to facilitate understanding') (see Yuan et al., 2020 and Chapters 1 and 5).

Reviewing this smörgåsbord with the students, they can realize how they have been influenced by different voices, but also how incompatible some of these ideologies are. What the students do with these critiques, is, in a sense, their 'problem'; however, we believe that they need to be aware of this range of ideologies, their origins, how they relate to systems of domination, their polysemy and potential compatibility. In our teaching, we do not support or put forward any of these ideologies as being the 'right ones' when we teach – although, of course, we have preferred ideologies of interculturality – but support them in unthinking and rethinking the notion.

In his work on intercultural philosophy Nelson (2019: 6) summarizes well what we attempt to achieve with our students: his wish is to reveal 'the multiperspectivality and multi-directionality of thinking' of interculturality. By learning to systematically ask questions such as 'What concepts and notions do we use to "do" and talk about interculturality?', 'What is the archaeology of these terms around the world?', 'Who proposed them/introduced them to discuss interculturality?' and 'What political motivations are behind them?' we argue that the students can start revising and adding to unproblematized ideologies of interculturality and thus enrich their worldviews.

'Can we be good at interculturality?'

The data used in this chapter consist of 37 short essays (maximum number of words per essay: 300) written by 3rd-year Bachelor's students in education at MUC. The essays were written in English, one of the languages used in the course. Our main motivation for asking them to use this international language was to see if the students attempted criticality and reflexivity in the way they discussed interculturality in a (global) language. Collected as part of a 16-week course on intercultural and Minzu education, the essays were written six weeks after the beginning of the course, in order to examine how the students took onboard the ideas that were shared and discussed around the three steps that form the backbone of the course. The essay title was: 'Can we be good at interculturality?' This broad and somewhat provocative question was meant to evaluate how the students invested the three steps to provide answers to the question. Since the essays were meant to be short, we do not claim that their contents reveal their full perceptions and ideological construction of the notion of interculturality. The next chapter explores their long-term engagement with critical perspectives on interculturality. However, we argue that there is a lot we can learn from the essays since they can allow us to observe (potential) change as it happens.

The course was taught by the authors in both Chinese and English (three hours per week). The group of students was composed of male and female students (approximately half-half) and 60 per cent of the students were from Minzus other than the Han Minzu. During the first six weeks of the course the following topics were dealt with: 1 What is interculturality?; 2 Is culture still a relevant concept?; 3 Identity and interculturality; 4 Imaginaries of interculturality; 5 Othering; 6 Pre-modernity, Modernity and Postmodernity.

The data was analysed by means of a thematic analysis (Braun & Clarke, 2006), which allows us to identify and report patterns (themes) within the data. The following analytical elements were used for each essay: What is the main argument of the essay? Are there contradictions between some of the arguments and assumptions? What concepts are introduced by the students? Are they explained and problematized? Do they use examples and illustrations to support their arguments? Are there any elements of Chineseness and/or Chinese Minzus used?

Analysis

Based on the thematic analysis of the 37 texts written by the students the analysis is composed of two main sections: 1 Factors contributing to 'being good (or not) at interculturality' and 2 How to develop interculturality? Each section contains the following subsections: 1a On the need to develop knowledge about interculturality, b. Role of the Structure; 2a Discourses of benevolence, b Multifaceted use of the concept of culture.

Let us share some general comments about the texts that we have analysed: First, amongst all the texts, the vast majority answered 'yes' to the question of 'Can we be good at interculturality?'. Although some of the students started by stating that it is a difficult question, they often were able to provide a (more or less convincing) answer. Student 31's answer was the most 'open' answer. He used a Chinese phrase to explain why he thinks that 'we can be good at interculturality':

Excerpt 1 – Student 31

I think that everyone can be good at it if he/she holds the belief of love, the idea of understanding and the expectation of a better world. So do we. There is a Chinese proverb that goes: Attitude decides everything. With this attitude, I am sure we have accomplished the half, as for the rest, just leave it to diligence and creativity. I don't think this can be done overnight, nor can it be done in a hurry.

For this student, interculturality relates to some sort of philosophy of life based on the values of 'love' and 'hope'. Introducing the Chinese phrase 态度决定一切 (*Attitude decides everything*), he insists first and foremost on the centrality of one's stance and mindset, and then on the role of chance, 'accident'. What the student argues throughout his essay is that one cannot program being 'good' at interculturality, and that interculturality takes time (see: 'I don't think this can be done overnight, nor can it be done in a hurry').

Only one student answered a clear 'no' to the question:

Excerpt 2 – Student 32

My answer is 'no'. Because everyone has a different identity, and it is a dynamic process of change at different times. With identity comes identity politics.

The student's argument relies on a discussion of the concept of identity which he uses as a way of questioning what he claims to be general assumptions about interculturality as a 'solid' process. We'll come back to this aspect in the next sections.

Second, very few students used examples or illustrations to justify their views about 'being good at interculturality'. Among the four students who did, three linked their answers to their own life experiences (e.g. someone they met) and one student to the scientific literature about expressing emotions.

Third, while analysing the data we had to negotiate the meaning of what the students were trying to say at times. Words such as *objective*, *development*, and *cross-cultural* often appeared in English in the texts but seemed to have unstable signifiers. They had to be discussed so that we would not mis-interpret the data. Let us provide an example from Student 35:

Excerpt 3 – Student 35

Eliminating the inherent prejudice and actively conducting cultural self-examination through others are more conducive to promoting development.

The word *development* is used with different meanings in the students' texts to describe, for example, the process in which something becomes more advanced (economically), an event representing a new stage in a situation, but also – as is the case in this excerpt – an experienced process of change in someone. The use of the first meaning by the students is the most common to discuss interculturality in Minzu contexts, probably due to the fact that many discussions around Minzu issues relate to, for example, economic development (see Sude et al., 2020). In Chinese the word for development, 发展, translates as 'becoming different', and contains the characters for 'hair' and 'to spread out'(发) as well as 'show'/exhibition (展). It is also noteworthy that many students seem to use the English words 'cross-cultural' and 'intercultural' interchangeably in their texts. After checking the Chinese for both words, we realized that there is only one word in this language to refer to these two notions: 跨文化. Although in English there might be differences between *cross-cultural* and *intercultural*, they can also refer to the same realities in some contexts and for some decision-makers, educators and scholars.

Finally, some students used what we refer to as *interculturalspeak* (Dervin, 2016) in their answers, that is, a somewhat automatic 'robot-like' way of talking about interculturality by using phrases, mottos/slogans and words that are not critically or reflexively evaluated. In some of the texts, we also noted gentle clashes of ideologies which will be discussed in the following sections.

Factors contributing to 'being good' (or not) at interculturality

On the need to develop knowledge about interculturality

One of the first common themes that appears in the essays is that of the need felt by the students to be knowledgeable about interculturality to be able to be 'good' at it. This aspect might relate to the fact that the data was collected as part of a theoretical course on the notion. Student 1 shares the view in this first excerpt:

Excerpt 4 – Student 1

In the face of more and more diverse areas of cultural contact, we need to improve our theoretical level of interculturality, that is, in terms of guiding principles, we should know how to communicate and connect with people from different cultural backgrounds.

Using an argument revolving around the concept of *culture* ('diverse areas of cultural contact', 'people from different cultural backgrounds'), the student insists on the need to acquire 'guiding principles' (a synonym for theories?) about interculturality. Student 8 in Excerpt 5 goes deeper into what needs to be learned by listing concepts that also derive from the concept of culture:

Excerpt 5 – Student 8

We inevitably need to be familiar with various related concepts, such as cultural identity, cultural discrimination, cultural infiltration and so on. These are the major obstacles for us to learn cross-culturally well. Only when we can fully understand the connotation of cross-cultural and related concepts and form our own theoretical system, can we be conducive to cross-cultural learning.

Amongst the three listed concepts only cultural identity was discussed during the lectures, the other two concepts of cultural discrimination and cultural infiltration, which are often used in relation to Minzu, are introduced by the student herself. While cultural discrimination might be self-explanatory, cultural infiltration (or penetration, 文化渗透) is a concept used in Chinese to refer to a 'strong culture' influencing a 'less powerful one', which could be translated as 'cultural invasion' although the word *invasion* is too strong compared to what the Chinese version connotes. What is interesting about what the student affirms here is that she considers that these concepts can be counter-productive if one does not learn to 'fully understand' them and what they connote – or even act upon the phenomena they describe. As mentioned in the first part of this chapter, we had spent time with the students discussing this important aspect of interculturality. About theoretical learning, Student 19 argues that having access to knowledge produced in other parts of the world ('overseas' in the excerpt) can help to decentre in relation to interculturality:

Excerpt 6 – Student 19

I need to take a more distant view of learning, to learn overseas empirical theories, or even to visit other countries to learn.

While increasing one's theoretical knowledge about interculturality is argued for by many students, others consider the development of technology and fast movement of humans and goods from one place to another to be beneficial to developing interculturality. In what follows, Students 5 and 11 discuss the importance of information technology (the Internet):

Excerpt 7 – Student 5

In today's highly developed information technology, the Internet has broken through the limitation of time and space and greatly narrowed the distance between people, especially between different cultural groups. This kind of condition gives us more opportunities to understand other cultures and greatly reduces the possibility of stereotyping.

Excerpt 8 – Student 11

With the development of Internet technology and the improvement of people's general education level, we have more opportunities for more and more people to open up their horizons and to have a more objective and comprehensive understanding of cultural differences and similarities, thus avoiding, for example, the negative impact of a single story.

In these excerpts both students seem to define what interculturality entails and thus the ways technology can support 'being good at it': (Student 5) 'understand other cultures and greatly reduces the possibility of stereotyping'; (Student 11) 'open up their horizons and to have a more objective and comprehensive understanding of cultural differences and similarities, thus avoiding for example, the negative impact of a single story'. For them, interculturality should lead to having a more objective and comprehensive understanding of 'cultures' and reducing stereotyping ('single story'). Technology seems to be leading us to achieve these aspects according to the students. A note on the use of the adjective 'objective' is needed at this stage. Many students use it in their texts when they describe what 'good at interculturality' means to them. In the Chinese word for *objective*, 客观, the first character refers to *a customer* (*subjective* contains the character for *the Lord* 主). What the students seem to mean here is that by providing access to and showing different realities, technologies can transform people's perceptions from the 主 *Lord* view (Self) to the 客 *customer* perspective (the 'Other'). Therefore, for the students in this section, knowledge about interculturality consists in decentring oneself from what one (thinks one) knows by experiencing theoretical knowledge and examining other realities.

In a similar vein, for Student 29 direct contact established by transport (travel?) improves 'being good at interculturality':

Excerpt 9 – Student 29

The development of transportation technology promotes cross-regional cultural exchange, and the emergence of information technology even turns the earth into a village in the network. These technologies give us the opportunity and ability to learn more about other cultures.

Although these excerpts emphasize the importance of reflecting on knowledge and different realities, somewhat blinded by our misperceptions, we note that the students are sometimes too idealistic (e.g. use of the cliché of 'information technology even turns the earth into a village') or lack criticality for example in relation to the use of the concept of *culture* or to the kind of knowledge that one could acquire from other countries. What is more, the argument about information technology and the somewhat illusionary argument of the 'contact hypothesis' (Allport, 1954) – that is, contact between people, face-to-face or online is enough to trigger interculturality – would need to be unthought and rethought with the students.

Role of the structure

This section is based on the students' inclusion of what we refer to as the Structure in how they determine the possibility of 'being good at interculturality'. The Structure here corresponds to what Althusser calls Ideological State Apparatuses (2001), which determine a system of production relations in which people live. For the philosopher these include two kinds of Apparatuses: 1 The ones which function by violence (e.g. courts, the police, prisons, the army); 2 Ideological state Apparatuses such as religion, education, politics, trade unions, the media, the arts. These function by ideology and tell us to think and act in the interests of the economic dominance of the ruling class. In addition to these Apparatuses, Global Ideological Apparatuses also have an influence on the way we think about 'us' and 'them'. People have no choice but to submit freely to all these Apparatuses in the interests of the economy – even if some might show signs of resistance. In the students' texts the following components of the Structure are included: the economy, supranational political institutions and the generic Apparatus of 'countries'. It is important to note that the students never mention concrete 'actors'.

The first excerpt from Student 4 is the most comprehensive in terms of the role of the Structure in promoting interculturality. In fact, the whole text oscillates between discourses around the following Apparatuses: 'countries', the economy and supranational political institutions. The excerpt starts with a comment on countries, then moves to the economy, diplomacy and 'people-to-people exchanges', to conclude with the economy (and a direct reference to 'economic theory'):

Excerpt 10 – Student 4

One country that is good at cross-cultural communication is dynamic and active, rather than complacent and backward.

The interaction and innovation brought by communication can improve the development space and comprehensive competitiveness of a country.

Cross-cultural communication will also have a greater impact on economic and trade, and play a more significant positive role in diplomatic development, international status, international tourism and people-to-people exchanges.

Cross-regional, cross-national, cross-polity and cross-national communication is associated with certain risks. However, it is pointed out in economic theory that risks and benefits coexist.

For the student, countries must be 'dynamic', 'active', 'competitive', 'international' and 'risk-taking' in order to create interculturality. The position of people is limited in this excerpt as the contexts introduced by the student remain at a macro-level.

Student 36 focuses mostly on the personal level in her essay but comments on the responsibility of one Apparatus:

Excerpt 11 – Student 36

First of all, this is a personal issue as well as an international issue, as it involves all regions and everyone. The relevant political institutions should also establish an exchange strategy for the peaceful coexistence of various ethnic cultures.

The Apparatus, 'the relevant political institutions', is deemed in charge of making sure that interculturality takes place 'peacefully'. For the student, interculturality, from this macro-perspective, translates as 'the peaceful coexistence of various ethnic cultures'. All the words in this 'definition' hint at the influence of a certain understanding of Minzu communication. The use of the concept of 'ethnic cultures' (which would not be used in many contexts around the world) is a strong indicator of this influence. We note that this student does not refer to any economic aspects in his text.

The last excerpt of this section contains a critique of certain 'countries and nations'. The critique relates to their roles in 1 creating a sense of ethnocentrism amongst their people while 2 Looking down upon others by creating what the student labels 'stereotypical images of other cultures' as well as 'mutual incomprehension and non-acceptance':

Excerpt 12 – Student 10

In my opinion, there are two factors that make us not very good at interculturality: firstly, there are objective political factors, where countries or nations may try to strengthen their internal unity and cohesiveness by making their own nation or nationality more visible and slightly less visible to other nations or nations, or by giving more negative information about other cultures to their own people. This, coupled with the fact that exchanges between cultural groups are not as close as those within one's own nation, is likely to lead to stereotypical images of other cultures, thus deepening mutual incomprehension and non-acceptance.

For the student, such Apparatuses need to contribute to making interculturality inclusive, critical of limited images of Self and the 'Other', and provide *objective* information about the 'Other'.

This section focused on how some students construct discourses about the role of the Structure on the possibility of 'being good at interculturality' – shifting the focus from the individual to the forces of political, economic and ideological Apparatuses. Together with the first analytical subsection about the need to develop knowledge about interculturality, this section demonstrates that some students are able to identify what factors could contribute (or not) to being 'good' at interculturality. We have noted some definitions of the notion in the excerpts, and a somewhat overreliance on the concept of *culture*. In what follows, we examine how the students suggest developing 'being good at interculturality'.

How to develop interculturality?

Discourses of benevolence

In the vast majority of the students' texts many keys to 'being good at interculturality' fall within a category that we label *benevolence*, the quality of being well-intentioned, kindness. The phrases used by the students are often found in the international literature on interculturality: *avoid conflict, end discrimination, break down stereotypes, put an end to ethnocentrism*. We also identified references to the verbs *to respect* and *to tolerate* in many sentences that appeared to read like mottos or slogans – without being problematized: 'First, we must learn to respect and tolerate' (Student 18); 'Second, respect and tolerate others' (Student 23). The use of the verb *to accept* seems to serve the same purpose and to also be used in a fluid way: 'we must accept cultural differences' (Student 33); 'we should sincerely and tolerantly recognize and accept each other's similarities and differences' (Student 25). In these two excerpts, we note a slight 'clash' of ideologies since Student 33 suggests 'accepting cultural differences' while Student 25 reported 'each other's similarities and differences', without the word *culture* and within the continuum of differences and similarities – instead of what Dervin (2016) has referred to as the 'differentialist bias'.

In Excerpt 13, Student 2 focuses on stereotypes and explains what 'breaking them down' means:

Excerpt 13 – Student 2

We should break down stereotypes, look at people without coloured glasses, tear off the labels and define a person by his own characteristics rather than his own cultural characteristics.

Metaphors ('coloured glasses', 'labels') are used to introduce the idea that one should move away from 'culture' to focus on the individual. Although this excerpt contains a modal verb ('should'), other assertions made by the students about benevolence are formulated in peremptory sentences, like orders. Excerpt 14 introduces critical discourses about the concept of *culture* (see next section) to lead to the conclusion of avoiding 'evils' of intercultural encounters such as discrimination and racism:

Excerpt 14 – Student 12

I agree with this view: culture is neither bounded nor closed; it is not homogeneous; it is the result of human being's generation, acquired postnatally (through education, etc.), meeting and integrating with other cultures in the long history.

Therefore, we need to avoid similar situations and avoid discrimination, racism and stereotype in intercultural communication.

Student 34, who shares very similar views, even provides a personal narrative to describe how she has herself experienced being prejudiced against certain representatives of other nations, showing a good level of reflexivity and self-criticality:

Excerpt 15 – Student 34

When I was a child, my mom had dinner with a Japanese gentleman and I expressed my hate after knowing his nationality. Every time I record this with a strong sense of shame. He is really a gentleman, but I tag him 'bad guy' because of his nationality.

In the final excerpt, Student 17 illustrates his reflections on similarities and differences between himself and another Chinese of Tibetan background and one of us who was teaching on the course – a 'Caucasian':

Excerpt 16 – Student 17

Whether it is to associate with Professor Fred, who is far away in Finland, or with the Mongolian student sitting next to me, it belongs to cross-cultural communication for me. Perhaps someone will immediately refute me, arguing that Fred and I come from totally different cultural backgrounds, but my Mongolian classmates are at least Chinese.

I would like to ask a question: when I associate with Fred, am I dealing with people from all over Finland? Of course not. I'm just associating with him. It has nothing to do with other Finns. In this case, why should I use the cultural label 'Finland' to define Fred in advance and think that our communication will be more difficult?

If we need to divide them according to some standards, it is obvious that Fred and I are humorous people (although sometimes we may accidentally tell some frost jokes), but the Tibetan student around me is serious. If we want to identify ourselves according to some kind of identity, can Fred and I enter a 'humor circle' and exclude this Tibetan student?

What the student shows here is his awareness that interculturality does not necessarily refer to cross-border encounters but that it also applies to locality. He gives the examples of Mongolian classmates and a Tibetan student, whom he compares to the foreign professor. In the second paragraph of the excerpt the student shows a good level of reflexivity by asking questions to himself about how to treat these different individuals, especially the Caucasian professor – hinting at the fact that he wishes to avoid generalizing and stereotyping representatives of the professor's country. The third paragraph contains the identification of a similarity with the foreign professor ('humour') which is opposed to the 'seriousness' of the Tibetan student. So, intercultural comparison thus moves beyond the 'international-based' understanding of interculturality to be applied to locality.

In this section, we have demonstrated that there are signs of the students wishing to show benevolence towards the 'Other' through respecting, tolerating and avoiding stereotyping. Some of the students were also navigating within the continuum of difference-similarity with the 'Other'. Maybe the aspect that seems to be missing here is the expectation of reciprocity in terms of how one treats the 'Other'. If one tolerates them, avoids using stereotypes against them (if that's possible), should we not expect the 'Other' to do the same? Can these acts of benevolence just be a one-way phenomenon?

Multifaceted use of the concept culture

In this last analytical version, we focus on the concept of culture, which is commented upon systematically in all the 37 texts that we collected. Some of the students were very critical of the concept, emphasizing its fluid character and commenting upon issues of identity, while a minority of students used culturalist discourses – culture as the only explanatory force to encounters, see Chemla & Keller, 2017 – to determine how to 'be good at interculturality'. Two students' texts were clearly culturalist:

Excerpt 17 – Student 25

But I'm aware of the importance of the interculturality research, cultural differences and the cultural collision is fundamentally caused by cultural differences, so respect is different from the native culture of foreign culture is the basis of interculturality communication, respect and open mind is a start, because they do not understand each other's national cultural taboos and misunderstandings.

Excerpt 18 – Student 34

I think everyone can be good at interculturality. In interculturality, we often have conflict because we are not familiar with other's culture background.

In Excerpt 18, Student 25 uses the word culture and its companion terms throughout: 'cultural differences' (twice), 'cultural collision', 'foreign culture' and 'national cultural taboos'. Culture is clearly seen as a problem and as something that leads to misunderstandings (amongst others). Student 34 also emphasizes the negative side of culture leading to 'conflict'.

Other students are very critical of the concept. The three following students use metaphors to describe what they see as problems in the use of the concept: (Excerpt 20) 'imprisoned in the "straitjackets" of culture'; (Student 27) 'confine ourselves in a certain cultural shackles' (sic); (Student 32) "blindfolded cultural label". For them, removing these problematic aspects of culture in the way interculturality is done represents potential paths towards being 'good at' it.

Excerpt 19 – Student 26

As culture has always been at the centre of discussions in intercultural education and people remain imprisoned in the 'straitjackets' of culture.

Excerpt 20 – Student 27

We live in a global village, rather than confine ourselves in a certain cultural shackles, overestimate or underestimate ourselves or others from a cultural perspective, but take an equal attitude towards each person's cultural background.

Excerpt 21 – Student 32

If we can tear off the blindfolded 'cultural label' and treat every communication as a complete 'risk equality' attempt, we can conduct cross-cultural communication more objectively and sincerely.

In a similar vein, Student 9 – in a somewhat imperious manner, however – asserts that the concept cannot be used because it 'isolates' and creates 'many prejudices and ideologies':

Excerpt 22 – Student 9

Trying to flout a culture or its boundaries often leads to isolation from a world with which it interacts and that influences it. When we use the concept of culture, we are often influenced by many prejudices and ideologies, so we can't use the concept of culture correctly.

The use of the first-person pronoun of the plural (we) adds to the student's strong conviction about the concept. Student 30 also takes a position against culture, suggesting to 'ignore' it although she still seems to give it some importance as 'one of the possible factors':

Excerpt 23 – Student 30

But this is obviously not an easy thing, because the best way of interculturality communication is to ignore culture. Culture is not the result or the main factor, but one of the possible factors.

The fluid characteristic of culture is noted many a times by the students. In Excerpt 22 the student is categorical about the fact that culture is a construction, taking place through encounters with 'other cultures' – thus personifying culture, giving it agency:

Excerpt 24 – Student 21

Interculturality expresses a simple truth: culture constructs itself through its relationships. It also constitutes itself through the relationship with other cultures.

The constructivist perspective on culture is also commented on by a student who reflects on what can be learned from the Chinese word 文化 (culture):

Excerpt 25 – Student 28

Because the original meaning of 'Hua' is to change, generate and create.

The idea that culture is 'open' was also identified in Student 7's text, where he comments on the performative characteristic of the concept:

Excerpt 26 – Student 7

Culture is not the attribution of certain behaviour, but the performance of behaviour. Trying to define culture or its boundaries often leads to its closure and isolation from the world.
   It makes you think that you belong to a single nation, but the reality is that your body has more resonance with the world. Not only can a person's mind be diverse, but a person's body is also diverse. An open world begins with an open mind.

The excerpt starts with a critique of the tendency to delimit culture and thus to close it down and isolate it. The student continues with a metaphor about body/mind in relation to culture to discuss the openness and resonance of people with the world, rather with a single (national) culture.

For many students, discourses of culture and especially cultural difference are substituted with discussions of identity as change:

Excerpt 27 – Student 13

Culture is the laziest excuse to explain differences. In order to achieve smooth cross-cultural communication, each individual in cross-cultural communication should look at each other from the perspective of development, instead of defining each other rudely with simple stereotypes. The identity of an individual is diversified and constantly formed, rather than fixed and limited by culture.

This excerpt starts with a provocative statement about culture (it is 'the laziest excuse to explain differences'), and moves towards discussing interculturality as a process (the student uses the word 'development') and opposes identity as 'diversified and constantly formed' to culture which is said to be 'fixed and limited'.

For some of the students, the idea that the Self is constructed by the presence and in interaction with the 'Other' (and vice versa) is amply discussed. Student 9 asserts that:

Excerpt 28 – Student 9

Because it is through the eyes of the other that the self is constructed and our identity becomes alive.

Finally, Student 14 – like many other students – insists on the need to consider both similarities and differences between people from different countries. Using research from the field of communication, the student explains that many similarities had been identified in terms of facial expressions for basic emotions:

Excerpt 29 – Student 14

For example, studies of cross-cultural categories of facial expressions show that in American, European, South American and Asian cultures, people perceive in the same way eight different basic emotions – excitement, joy, surprise, sadness and pain, disgust, contempt, anger, shame and fear.

This section examined the presence of discourses of culture in the students' essays. Since a lot of discussions around the concept took place during the first six weeks of the course, it is not perhaps surprising that most students commented upon it. Although a couple of students seemed to share very strong culturalist positions what the other students seem to reveal is a good critical and reflexive stance towards the concept when discussing interculturality. Their discussions of identity as a fluid phenomenon complemented their critiques of culture and showed some awareness of, for example, the continuum of similarity-difference and the importance of change in interculturality.

[Pause]

In this chapter we used the notion of interculturality as an entry point into how Chinese students at an institution of higher education focusing on Minzu issues express, construct and discuss diversity when they answered the question 'Can we be good at interculturality?'. Several research questions were asked and our analytical sections provided the following answers: 1 The students were able to identify some factors contributing to 'being good at interculturality', including increasing one's knowledge of intercultural encounters and learning through today's intercultural facilitators such as digital technologies. Some students also emphasized the central role of the Structure ('ideological Apparatuses') at the local and global levels; 2 Suggestions – which often sounded like 'orders' – were also provided by the students. These included: somewhat typical 'global' discourses of benevolence relating to tolerance, respect, acceptance and putting an end to stereotyping. Although these are of importance, the fact that they were rarely problematized by the students (what does *tolerating* mean?) and not considered from the perspective of reciprocity made them rather empty proposals. Finally, the last analytical section reviewed the multifaceted use of the concept of *culture* by the students to answer the question of 'being good at interculturality'. While there were hints of culturalism (culture as a solid and static 'thing' used to explain the 'Self' and the 'Other', see Abdallah-Pretceille, 2004), the vast majority were critical of the concept and pushed for a more fluid and constructivist understanding.

In the course that the students were taking, we had introduced a three-step model of interculturality: 1 Deconstructing the smörgåsbord of ideologies about interculturality; 2 Reviewing the terms used to discuss interculturality; and 3 Opening up to alternative ideologies. While the students were only in their sixth week of the course (reminder: this was a 16-week course) there were signs that the students were already able to demonstrate that they possessed some of these subcompetences. As far as 'deconstructing the smörgåsbord of ideologies about interculturality' is concerned, some students were able to identify the influence of global/local systems of politico-economic institutions and of global dominating ideologies. A few students also discussed some of the 'ought tos' and 'orders' from these institutions (e.g. the imposition of discourses of culture leading to prejudice and stereotypes). The objectives of 'reviewing the terms used to discuss interculturality' and 'opening up to alternative ideologies' were marginally found in the data. As such, very few students proposed multilingual and 'archaeological' analyses of concepts and notions (one student mentioned the word *culture* in Chinese and its original connotation of change, see Fang, 2019). Finally, although many of the proposed ideas represented alternative ideologies about interculturality, they were still somewhat grounded in Western-centric worldviews. As such, postmodern discourses around identity were used by some students, but it is important to bear in mind that the idea of identity as a fluid phenomenon (although it may not be framed this way) is omnipresent in past and present conceptualizations of the 'Self' and the 'Other' in many parts of the world (see 论语, the Analects of Confucius).

What seems to be missing in the students' texts – which would require further work with them in the future (and will be addressed in the next chapter) – comprises:

- The lack of deep engagement with Minzu and Chinese ideologies about diversity and interculturality could be explained by the fact that the texts were produced in English, requiring the students to think (maybe) in a specific mind-world. Although we identified some traces and signs (some 'slogans' and the use of some particular terms), there would be a need for them to be further considered and problematized against other ideologies.
- Many of the proposed answers to the question 'Can we be good at interculturality?' resemble slogans and mottos in the sense that they are not discussed but just 'thrown in' the students' texts. They would need to be more explicitly discussed and critiqued.
- The essay instructions did not ask the students to illustrate their arguments by use of examples. Yet it would be important for them to be able to systematically use some to make their arguments more convincing and concrete at times.
- During the course the students are urged to look at the words they use in Chinese and English to talk about interculturality reflexively and critically. Very few scholars have suggested that such multilingual perspectives be systematically included in intercultural education but we do believe, based on our own cooperation as a multilingual team, that such work is necessary and rewarding to unthink and rethink interculturality.

All in all, while reading and analysing the students' data, we felt that they were experiencing some changes – more or less consciously – in the way they perceive, construct and discuss interculturality. More explicit and metacognitive work about the form and content of discourses about interculturality is needed. However, we note, with one of the students from this research, that a multi-ideological notion like interculturality, which looks like Henry James's complex figure in a Persian carpet, requires lifelong engagement: 'I don't think this can be done overnight, nor can it be done in a hurry'.

[Time to reflect]

- How would you answer the question 'Can we be good at interculturality?'. Discuss some of the arguments presented by the students in this chapter.

- At this stage in the book, how many perspectives from the smörgåsbord of interculturality are you able to name and problematize (including local perspectives)?

- What do you make of the two concepts of *culture* and *civilization*? What do they mean to you? What do you think influenced the way(s) you use them when you talk about interculturality?

- One student from the study used this phrase to describe how we should deal with interculturality: 态度决定一切 (*Attitude decides everything*). What are your views on this?

- Another student suggested 'looking at people without coloured glasses' as an objective for interculturality. What did he mean?

- Based on the definition of the concept of *ideology* that we use in this chapter, we argued that 'ideology' refers to a system of ideas elaborated on in the light of certain conceptions of what 'ought to be'. Explain why interculturality in education cannot escape from ideologies.

- Do you consider 'cultural infiltration' or 'penetration' (文化渗透) to be a problem? Can you give some examples?

- Does the generalized use of the Internet around the world promote interculturality? Why (not)?

Note

1 The Hui people mainly come from Northwest China and the Zhongyuan region.

5 Minzu as an entry into the smörgåsbord of interculturality

'Our university is an ideal place to study and work. We will enhance democracy as well as genuine and empathic diversity in the work community, which stems from respect for and the willingness to support each member of the university community.' These words were uttered at the beginning of the new academic year at a European institution of higher education, ranked among the 50 best universities in the world. The words 'democracy' and 'diversity' are used to support the argument that this institution is 'ideal' for 'every member of the community' who studies and works there. This type of speech is not exceptional since we have heard it uttered in very similar ways in other higher education institutions around the world (Australia, Canada, China, France, Great Britain, Japan, Malaysia, etc.). In order to fulfill this 'contract' of democracy and inclusion of diversity, most universities offer 'intercultural courses' (among others) to support inclusion, intercultural dialogue and the creation of 'authentic internationalization' (Dervin, Härkönen, Yuan, Chen, & Zhang, 2020). In this chapter, we name this multifaceted phenomenon ICE.

ICE is provided in different departments and faculties such as linguistics, education, business schools, nursing education (Tournebise, 2012). The titles of courses on intercultural issues can also be diverse and varied in the world, even in the same country and the same institution: *intercultural, multicultural, transcultural, diverse* and *global*. These courses can be intended for so-called 'local' students, international and exchange students, but also for teachers/researchers and administrative staff. Finally, those who teach it are either specialists of the field or non-specialists but, who through their backgrounds or their scientific affiliations (e.g. language education), are led to improvise as teachers of interculturality (Tournebise, 2012).

This field of research and practice is thus complex, both in the variety of interventions and in terms of content. In his *Abécédaire*, when he talks about his book on the fold, Deleuze (1996) shares his surprise at the letters that he received after the book was published. Letters from a club

DOI: 10.4324/9781351044554-6

of origamists (who, through folding and sculpting, transform a sheet of paper into a finished model) and surfers (among others) gave him the impression that all these readers had read his book on a particular phenomenon (*the fold*) from their own interests and experiences and that they all claimed in their own way that 'the fold is me!' (Deleuze, 1996). ICE appears at first glance as Deleuze's fold too.

In this chapter, we problematize this area of education based on the experiences of our team composed of Chinese and Finnish researchers. Having had to teach interculturality to Chinese students at MUC, we reflected on the problems of *IEC as a fold* in this specific context. MUC represents what we call a 'microcosm of Chinese diversity'. Surprisingly, this unique context has led to very little research, particularly on questions of ICE (exceptions: Clothey & Hu, 2014). In a previous study (Yuan et al., 2020), we were able to demonstrate, however, that the Minzu approach used in this university allows students to explore both the diversity of China and of the world; to reflect on their identities; to cooperate and learn with students from other Minzus, who do not necessarily share their worldviews; and to develop a critical and reflexive sense towards meeting the 'Other'. We therefore suggested that this approach represented an important anti-hegemonic alternative to explore (ibid.), beyond the scholarship produced in the 'West', that has tended to denigrate it (ex: Postiglione, 2013; Yang, 2017).

Our team jointly delivered a course on ICE to a group of Chinese second-year education students (T = 17) for 12 weeks. In what follows, we start by problematizing the notion of interculturality in order to propose an approach that takes into account criticisms of ICE. We call this approach Critical and Reflexive Literacy of interculturality. Then, based on documents collected from our students during and after the course, we examine the influences of this approach on the way they discuss and conceptualize interculturality.

The intercultural as a variable ideology

From the beginning of our cooperation, we have chosen an intellectual position that we call *transpositions*. The Chinese notion of 换位 思考 inspired us to take this path. 换位 思考 can be translated in different ways: for example put yourself in the other person's shoes, mutual empathy and understanding and 换 means *to change*, 位 (*the*) *place* and 思考 *to think*. The idea of these transpositions between us was first of all to swap places: Researchers from the Finnish context specialize in interculturality while Chinese colleagues specialize in Minzu education. So, we started by examining our ways of talking about the phenomena we work on, the concepts and notions we use, our research results. During our preliminary dialogues, we noticed our similarities and divergences. The second stage of our transpositions consisted in negotiating and adapting these elements in order to organize the course in question. However, this step was difficult because negotiating elements marked by specific local contexts and discourses and by elements stemming from global discourses (which do not always go hand in hand) seemed to lead to contradictions but also to reinforce inequalities between us (which would have been unfair to the students). Indeed, as we were working in English, those of us from China tended to accept the Finnish team's points of view and to prefer the concepts and ideas that were brought by them (which were very 'Eurocentric'), abandoning what we considered to be more acceptable. This is how we decided together to change our approach: We no longer wanted to 'brainwash' students by means of our two approaches (or through a 'bad' hybrid version).

In what follows, we share the reflections that the 'silent transformation' (Jullien, 2010) that we have experienced has instilled. By silent transformation, we refer to this 'silent journey' (Jullien, ibid.), to this common awareness built through our dialogues, that ICE, in the specific context of MUC, should first help them question the concept of interculturality but, above all, identify ways of problematizing it around the world and in China.

Our first observation was that interculturality, but also Minzu, seem to ask themselves the same questions: 1 'What is a social being?'; 2 'What is meeting others and how to manage encounters?'; 3 'How to live with others?'

Reading these questions, it is clear that, in research and education, the answers we provide are always ideological, influenced by local, regional and international policies, but also by the beliefs and experiences of educators themselves. For Althusser (2001: 2), ideology is often overlooked as being ideological. He writes (ibid.): 'Ideology is never said to be ideological'. Therefore, these ideological aspects of interculturality lead to a smörgåsbord (Scandinavian buffet containing hot and cold foods) of beliefs, opinions and approaches, based on (amongst others) different concepts, notions, theories, paradigms, sometimes imposed by local economic and political structures. The metaphor used by Mannheim (1929/2006) to speak of ideology and utopia seems well suited to this context: the 'carousel of points of view'. However, as asserted earlier, these various ideological elements are also dominated by a certain international doxa on what/who represents interculturality and on how it should be dealt with.

ICE has been dominated by ideologies with an essentialist tendency, which operate hierarchies between individuals, for example, in terms of courage, honesty, politeness and punctuality. This is the case of culturalism, which makes the concept of culture (sometimes intersecting with the concepts of race and religion, in a disguised manner) a unique explanatory force, based on a national, modern and deterministic ideology (e.g. Wikan, 2006). The intercultural approaches of researchers such as Hall, Hofstede or Huntington, from the worlds of American diplomacy and politics and international trade, have helped to create this tenacious ideology and to impose ways of conceiving and speaking of ICE across the world (McSweeney, 2010). Thus, the idea of 'culture shock', the dichotomies of 'individualism' vs. 'collectivism', or the argument that ICE should allow students to get rid of their stereotypes by developing intercultural competence (see Byram, 2020, which is of course a utopia!), derive from culturalist approaches and represent ideologies that are found throughout the world in publications, curricula, political speeches, and so on.

Beyond culturalism, certain educational and research perspectives called 'critical' have also contributed to 'stereotyping' certain ideas or discourses on interculturality: biased comparisons between 'interculturalism' vs. 'multiculturalism' (with a preference for the first in Abdallah-Pretceille, 2004, supporting a certain ideological secularism); the naive belief in sincere intercultural transformation (see in Holliday, 2010 for example the idea that one can render an essentialist 'non-essentialist', a racist 'non-racist'); the idea that individuals can navigate from one identity to another as they wish (cf. Dervin, 2016 based on Bauman's liquid identity); and finally an approach focused on the individual, beyond interactions and relationships and the Structure that dominates them (see Ferri's review, 2018). All these elements also form the basis of ideologies and new 'commonplaces' (Ellul, 1966) that circulate around the world.

In addition to individual initiatives by researchers and practitioners who have had some international success (e.g. Byram, Hofstede or Holliday in English) or geopolitically distributed (e.g. Abdallah-Pretceille, Zarate in French-speaking worlds; Talib, Dervin in Finland; Yihong Gao in China), we note the primordial influence of supranational institutions in the creation of ideologies and of a certain doxa on interculturality. UNESCO, the Council of Europe but also the OECD, play an essential role in this 'ideological carousel'. These institutions have also imposed models of intercultural competence to the whole world: UNESCO relies on the work of the American scholar Darla Deardorff; the Council of Europe has been using the idea of the competence of democratic culture since 2018 as a substitute for the concept of the intercultural, based on the work of the British scholar Michael Byram; and the OECD, also building on the work of Deardorff, has been promoting a model of global competence since 2019. All these models are based on ideologies determined by the geo-economic-political contexts of these researchers (often: Great Britain, the United States), mixed with the economic-political ideologies of these institutions, and impose ways of speaking about interculturality. Indirectly this leads to judging those who practice interculturality on the basis of criteria which ignores other ideologies. Thus, the meeting of the 'Other' across the world is 'governed' by documents written in Paris and Strasbourg, France (headquarters of these institutions).

We also noted in the discussions between our teams that we were all aware and embarrassed by certain doxic elements of the intercultural which circulate in our contexts and greatly influence researchers, teachers and students. As we work in English, our references are often limited to a reduced space of thought, that of the research produced in this language and published in international journals from the *Social Sciences Citation Index* (SSCI) database in China or the *Julkaisufoorumi* (JUFO) in Finland. Of course, this space of thought is not homogeneous. However, the most prestigious bibliographical references circulate and impose inevitable ideologies. In a 2020 study, Peng et al. carried out a bibliometric analysis of publications on the concept of *intercultural competence* in English. We note that the five most cited researchers in their study (Byram, Deardorff, Kramsch, Hammer and Bennett) are all white, English-speaking, mostly American scholars (plus one Briton and a researcher born in France but who has spent their entire career in the United States since 1969). Even if their work differs a little ideologically (because of the different scientific, political and/or economic 'tribes' to which they belong), there are many similarities in their way of speaking about interculturality and in their choice of words, concepts and arguments. Through their influences in the world, numerous research and pedagogical approaches become facsimiles of their ideologies — even in contexts where these ideologies are contrary to local ideologies (see for example the use of Byram's (2008) 'hyper-European' concept of *intercultural citizenship* which is used in China, but emptied of the political connotations imposed by the Council of Europe). The production of knowledge on the intercultural then seems 'colonized' by these ideologies, which do not recognize themselves as ideologies but 'natural' ways of 'doing' the intercultural (Dervin & Simpson, 2021).

A proposal: a Critical and Reflexive Literacy of intercultural approaches

Any positioning on interculturality in education and research is ideological and brings no universal truth about what is intercultural or how to cope with it. As a consequence, it seems important to integrate the intersections between politics, the economy and research/education in our discussions of ICE, because choosing to teach interculturality leads to positioning ourselves in one of these approaches and to impose (in-) directly ideologies that are sometimes incompatible with the context of our students – or simply ideologies that are hardly acceptable. Tournebise (2012) clearly demonstrated how teachers of interculturality juggled opposite and often incompatible approaches in Finnish universities. In addition, these teachers were ignorant of the economic and political projects that hid behind the perspectives they used in their teaching. Finally, they were also unable to justify their preference for their approaches (Tournebise, ibid.). It is then easy to see the potential consequences that this can have on students.

This raises the question of teaching interculturality through the prism of ideologies, which could make the field more transparent, perhaps, less 'Westernized' and guided by cooperation less marked by a hierarchy of knowledge (e.g. 'East' and 'West'). There is actually very little research on this important issue. Indeed, many studies promote a specific approach (and therefore ideologies) (Spiteri, 2017; Shaules, 2019) while other studies evaluate the influence of these approaches on student learning (Jackson, 2018; Woodin, 2018).

Through our discussions and these reflections, we decided to orient our teaching towards more metacognitive work with our students. It was therefore not a question of choosing and favoring an intercultural approach (*Minzu*, *intercultural* or *global*, among others) which would 'format' the students but to offer the possibility of exploring different ideologies, of learning how to analyse them, and to decide about their value and usefulness. What we are proposing is called a Critical and Reflexive Literacy of Intercultural Approaches. Figure 5.1 shows the three closely related elements with which we have worked with our students. We use three metaphors to describe this model: *the fold*, *the handshake* and the *magic mirror*.

We briefly review these three aspects in what follows:

1   The fold is a direct reference to Deleuze's aforementioned remark. Similar to the complexity represented by the fold, the ideologies of interculturality are multiple, sometimes similar or different, sometimes largely influenced by the international. This is why we first had to train the students to identify the different orientations, ideologies and agendas behind any discourse and any perspective on interculturality. During the 12 weeks of the course, we therefore reviewed certain approaches drawn from educational and communication sciences, and analysed together the words and concepts used in each of them, in order to identify the underlying ideologies. This work was accom-

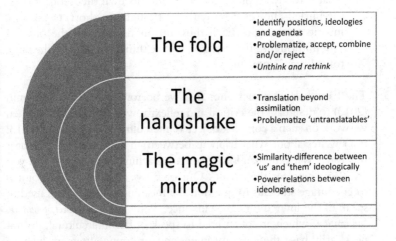

The fold	•Identify positions, ideologies and agendas •Problematize, accept, combine and/or reject •*Unthink and rethink*
The handshake	•Translation beyond assimilation •Problematize 'untranslatables'
The magic mirror	•Similarity-difference between 'us' and 'them' ideologically •Power relations between ideologies

Figure 5.1 A critical and reflexive literacy model of intercultural approaches

panied by discussions between the students and our team on what seemed to be acceptable, combinable and/or what should be rejected. Through these discussions and the awareness of the diversity of perspectives, processes of folding, unfolding and folding again were carried out. Elements of dialogical discourse analysis, which go beyond the surface of discourse and which allow ideologies to be identified, were very useful in making this work possible (Dervin, 2016).

2   The magic mirror is a Chinese invention dating back to the 5th century. Made of bronze, the mirror has two sides: one side with bronze designs and another, convex and polished, which serves as a mirror. When one holds the mirror in the sun, its reflective surface projects the bronze designs onto a surface (e.g. a white wall). One can look in the mirror and see what is printed on the other side. We use this metaphor to suggest the importance of observing both the differences and similarities between approaches to interculturality, from diverse contexts. At the same time, by looking at these elements in the mirror, we wanted the students to look at the ideological power relations between these approaches and the possible reasons for the 'stifling' of certain ideological voices. The approach of the philosopher and sinologist F. Jullien (2019: 6) is interesting in this sense:

> by organizing a vis-à-vis between Chinese and European thoughts, I make them reflect on each other, one by the other.

That is to say, to probe into the other its own theoretical biases, the buried choices from which it thought, in short, to go back into its unthought. Each thus 'un-builds' through the other. I call 'unthought', that from which we think and that, by the same token, we do not think.

3   The handshake is a metaphor that we borrow from Ross Benjamin (2013) to designate the critical and reflexive work of translation when we work on such a complex object as interculturality. Benjamin (2013: n.p.) writes about what happens between an author and a translator this way: 'With the handshake you are reaching out to them and you are also asking for their trust'. Our objective with this third point is to encourage students to question the meanings of the words used to speak of the intercultural. For instance, words such as *respect, tolerance, civilization,* which are often used to speak of the intercultural, do not necessarily have the same meanings and/or connotations in different languages. This is problematic because, when our students talk about the intercultural in English, the meaning they give to concepts and notions is not always contained in the words they use in English. Billeter (2006: 50) gives an interesting example from the Chinese word *tao*, which is often translated by *process* or *The Way*: 'In a dialogue imagined by the philosopher Tchouang-tseu, Confucius sees a swimmer frolicking at ease in tumultuous waters and then literally asks him, "Do you have a swimming tao?" The sinologist could translate by "Do you have a way of swimming?", but also, more simply, by "Is there a technique to swim?"' The handshake is thus about questioning, problematizing and creating connections between Chinese and English.

To sum up, the Critical and Reflexive Literacy of Intercultural Approaches that we propose leads students to not be satisfied with a single ideology that would be imposed on them, but to observe and study the diversity of ideologies of intercultural approaches, notably through translation and discourse analyses, and empower them to find new perspectives. Based on their findings, they can question their own beliefs and ideologies to determine, if possible, what seems personally acceptable, combinable or to be rejected in the approaches presented to them. The method leads to asking questions, without necessarily finding answers. It could nevertheless allow students to develop a critical sense in dealing with intercultural approaches. Table 5.1 presents the types of questions which can be asked when familiarizing ourselves with a specific intercultural approach.

Before examining how this Critical and Reflexive Literacy was taken into account by our students, we briefly describe the proposed

Table 5.1 Questions about intercultural approaches

Where does the approach come from?

How was it created and by whom? What information about the authors can you identify?

What political and economic influences? What ideologies?

What concepts are used in the approach? What definitions?

Do you know how to translate these concepts into other languages? What words are difficult to translate?

What are the problems with this approach in your context? Are the ideologies compatible with the ideologies of your country, of your institution?

How do people see these perspectives in other contexts?

What criticisms have been made of this intercultural model?

intervention. The bilingual introductory course (English/Mandarin Chinese) about interculturality and Minzu lasted 12 weeks, around two hours per week. Seventeen third-year education students participated in the course. Each week we discussed theoretical elements (definitions of concepts and notions, reviews of intercultural theories), models of inter-cultural competence (among others: Deardorff, Byram, Bennett), the contributions of different international and Chinese researchers, and the influence of supranational institutions (Council of Europe, UNESCO). At the beginning of the course, we asked the students to negotiate their own model of intercultural competence with each other, and to renegoti-ate it every two weeks. At the end of the course, we asked them to present their final model and to problematize it in connection with the theoreti-cal and methodological discussions of the course. The three aspects of the fold, the magic mirror and the handshake were systematically used to support the students in this revision work.

Many data were collected from the course and, within the limited framework of this chapter, we had to make a selection. In the following analysis, we offer an example illustrating each aspect of the Critical and Reflexive Literacy model: 1 An example of *the handshake* around concepts to use in English to rethink models of intercultural competence (week 5); 2 An example of *the magic mirror* through the final versions of the models produced by the students (week 12); 3 An example of *the fold* by analysing reflections written by the students six months after the end of the course. The data are mainly in English, with some in Chinese. While the first two examples are examined through descriptive content analy-sis (Neuendorf, 2017), the third example will be analysed by means of dialogical discourse analysis (Marková et al., 2012). The latter is inspired by the work of M. Bakhtin (1982) and the interdisciplinary movement, The Dialogical Self (Dervin, 2016) which observes the interweaving of multiple voices in the production of discourses. Linguistically speaking, this requires analysing the appearance and influence of elements such as pronouns, reported speeches, the use of the passive voice, the repetition of words (Dervin, ibid.).

An example of a conceptual handshake

Each week, we spent time with the students renegotiating the meaning of the words used in the theories and models we presented, as well as in what the students themselves produced and re-negotiated. During the fifth week, we paused to allow the students to present their models to others. This was followed by joint negotiation and building of a model of intercultural competence for the whole class. The end result of this work is not really of interest here (we shall look at the models of the different groups of students in the next section). However, the joint negotiations revealed important discussions around concepts and notions, in particular around translation and connotations.

After creating the common model, we asked the students to tell us which concepts, notions or goals should have been included. Table 5.2 presents these elements, which we classify into five categories:

Table 5.2 Concepts, notions and objectives to include

Category	Objectives
. . . around the concept of culture	Cultural confidence Cultural pride Sense of cultural identity Knowledge of Chinese culture More interaction around culture Learn about local culture
. . . around Minzu ideology	Minzu consciousness Diversity in unity Learn to deal with Minzu differences Create Minzu unity
. . . around an international ideology	Open-mindedness Respect Harmony How to deal with conflicts
. . . around the individual	Focus on individuals
. . . around language	Knowledge of different languages

Not surprisingly, the most important category is that of concepts, notions and objectives related to the idea of *culture*. This concept, as we have seen in previous chapters, has long been the anchor of intercultural research and teaching, even in China (ex: Holliday, 2010; Sude et al., 2020). Among the students' proposals, we can see that three concepts are put forward: *cultural confidence/pride*, and a sense of cultural identity. Three typical objectives are also proposed around culture: *knowledge of Chinese culture, more interactions around culture, learning about local culture*. Besides the fact that these elements are very similar to the ideologies of culturalism (Abdallah-Pretceille, 2004), we note however the appearance of the concept of *cultural confidence/pride* which led to many discussions between the students and our team. The meaning and ideology behind this expression may seem special, and problematic for some non-Chinese researchers and practitioners – stereotypically like some kind of 'fortune cookie slip' that makes no sense in English. The idea of trust and cultural pride seems to have its origins, in the Chinese context, in the speeches of Chinese President Xi, who, published an article in the magazine *Qiushi* (the bimonthly theoretical journal of the Communist Party of China) in June 2019, urging the Chinese to develop cultural trust, based on the principles of Marxism, and drawing inspiration from Ancient Chinese culture. In Chinese, the term translates as 文化 自信 (culture confidence). As stated before, the word *culture* (sometimes used as a synonym for civilization in English in China) is ambiguous in Chinese. In his book on the meaning of this concept in contemporary China, Fang (2019) shows how its meanings and connotations were influenced by the West during the years 1840–1900. Whereas, before, the word culture corresponded to its postmodern definition as something that is constantly changing and that is co-constructed between individuals, its meaning has become very close to that used by Western culturalists in the 20th century (Fang, ibid.). Nowadays, the word *culture* seems to be a floating signifier in Chinese, between culturalism and its more fluid postmodern version. This historical aspect led to discussions between the students and ourselves in order to become aware of its influence on translation.

The second category from the table comes directly from the ideologies of MUC around the notion of Minzu (see Yuan et al., 2020). The only concept present here is that of *awareness of Minzus*. The three proposed objectives come directly from the slogans and mottos promoted by the institution around the concepts of diversity and unity. This aspect goes beyond the 'culture' of the previous category and could have a more political meaning.

The third 'broad' category contains terms that are found in many approaches to ICE (see Byram, 2020): *openness, respect, conflict avoidance* and *harmony*. Two of these terms, which are sometimes used as empty signifiers in intercultural education (what do they really mean and for whom?), have led to 'handshake' discussions between the students and our team: *respect* and *harmony*. We discovered that, in Chinese, the idea of *respect* is polysemic and is expressed in at least two different ways: 尊重 (zunzhong) and 尊敬 (zunjing). While the first term refers to a polite meeting between individuals, who are marked by hierarchical differences such as an employer and an employee (= respect as a state to save face), 尊敬 (zunjing) would seem to represent a deeper phenomenon, which builds up as one meets each other (= respect as a process), and which would allow to go beyond a performance of 尊重 (zunzhong). During our discussions, the students agreed on the importance of 尊敬 (zunjing) to lead to *harmony*. It was then that another handshake discussion was launched around this term. While in some Western languages, the idea of relational harmony might seem 'solid', 'superficial' and 'performative', in Chinese, the word 和谐 (hexie) can describe a process of cooperation (和, re: together; 协, xie: cooperate), which seems to go well with the idea of 尊敬 (zunjing).

Some Sinologists or even Chinese speakers might disagree with these interpretations, which emerged from discussions with our students. However, what the handshake allows is to help the students: 1 Question the words ('untranslatables', Cassin, 2014) that they use in Chinese and English when they talk about interculturality; 2 Identify the ideological elements that make a word preferred or defined/understood in a certain way. This can allow students to learn to position themselves and to justify their choices among different ideologies. It is clear then that, depending on the translations used for the aforementioned terms, the objectives of interculturality can entirely change.

The magic mirror: students' models of intercultural competence

During the course, the students were able to observe and analyse different models of intercultural competence, while comparing the differences and similarities between these models and their ideological power relations. Over the weeks, we have tried not to impose our own views on the students but to support them in their critical and reflexive learning. During the last lecture, five groups of students, who had cooperated throughout the course, presented and justified the latest version of their model of intercultural competence. Among the five figures proposed by the students, two had been formulated in the form of lists of 'we can' components and three in the form of diagrams.

To begin with, we note that the figures of the five teams are relatively different. Some models seem to apply to general contexts of intercultural communication (groups 1, 2), while others focus on the specific context of MUC (groups 3, 4, 5). These diverse perspectives seem to correspond to an argument noted on the intercultural: it is a polysemic notion, with variable ideologies (Dervin, 2016). It is therefore not surprising that within one institution such as MUC, students produce different versions of this object of research and teaching.

The first two groups offer fairly similar elements around interaction with the 'Other', and mutual understanding. While the first group seems to focus on cultural aspects (see Figure 5.2: correctly understand different cultural speech and non-verbal behaviour; be familiar with cultural connotations; learn cross-cultural knowledge), the second group seems to go beyond the reference to culture (see Figure 5.3). In addition, we note that the first group often uses modalities to express the content of the

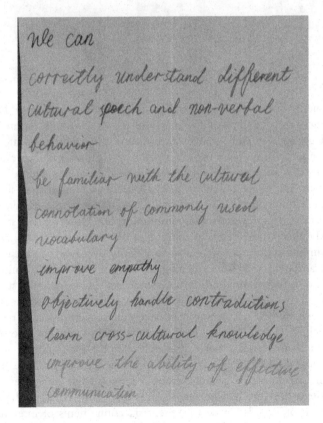

Figure 5.2 Group 1

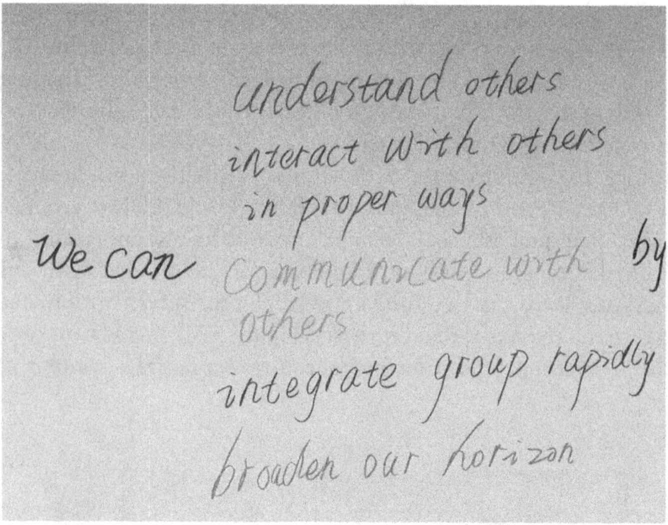

Figure 5.3 Group 2

components of the model: *correctly* (+ understand), *objectively* (+ handle contradictions), 'to improve the ability of *effective* communication'. The second group uses only one such modality in 'to communicate with others in *proper* ways'. We had discussed several times with the class the problems that the use of such subjective modal adverbs and adjectives (which we find in most Western models) could pose in terms of feasibility and reliability (Kerbrat-Orecchioni, 1994). Indeed, who decides what is 'correct' and/or 'objective' in communication? However, the students decided to keep these items. In addition to the elements linked to culture and communication, we were able to identify two aspects which could suggest an opening to other ideologies: '(objectively) handle contradictions' and 'broaden our horizon'. During class discussions, the students confirmed that these components were linked to the need to be critical and reflexive when talking about interculturality as an object of research and teaching. Through these two elements, the students include objectives which concern the metacognitive level of the intercultural.

The next models are presented more dynamically than the 'we can' lists from the previous two groups. Group 3 proposes five objectives, using the context of MUC to illustrate them (Figure 5.4). Group 4 draws on the design of a garden hose to present six components of intercultural competence, in the form of keywords (Figure 5.5). The last group uses

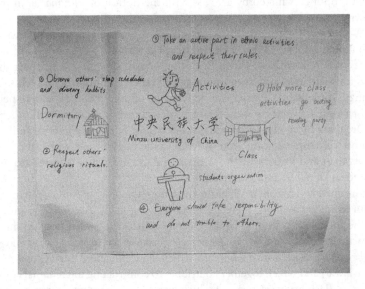

Figure 5.4 Group 3

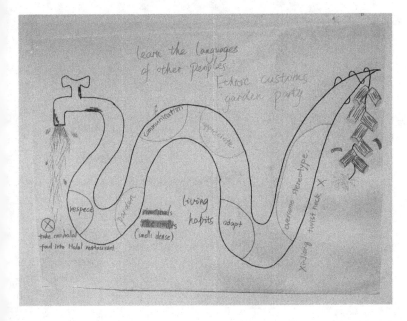

Figure 5.5 Group 4

five components linked by arrows (with the notion of *participation* in the centre) to explain the processes of interculturality (Figure 5.6).

We review each model in what follows. Group 3 poses the following principles: 1 Observe the habits of others in terms of sleep and food (students live in dormitories with five other Minzu students); 2 Respect the religious rituals of others (an indirect reference to Buddhist and Muslim Minzu students); 3 Participate actively in ethnic activities and respect their rules; 4 Everyone should take responsibility and not disturb others; 5 Organize more classroom activities (reading, outings). Here we find an almost verbatim reproduction of MUC's ideology, about which the students read and hear throughout their studies, and which centres around the ideas of *respect* and *active participation*.

Groups 4 and 5 seem to differ the most from the other groups by refraining from including a unique ideology about interculturality. According to group 4, the model starts from a 'liquid' metaphor, that of a garden hose, to show how their six keywords (*respect, forgiveness, communication, appreciate, adapt* and *go to (beyond stereotypes)*) are phenomena which 'flow' (therefore they are unstable, non-linear) and which together contribute to constructing intercultural competence. Each keyword, some of which have been used in previous models as well as in international models, is illustrated with an example to explain their

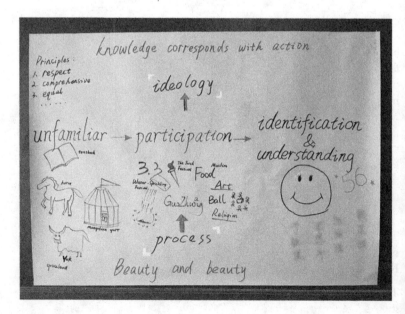

Figure 5.6 Group 5

meanings. For instance, the idea of going beyond stereotypes is illustrated by a reference to what the students call the 'Xinjiang twist neck' (i.e. 'head wobble'). Xinjiang is the largest autonomous region of China, predominantly Muslim. According to the students, a common representation of this community in China is that its members shake their heads when they speak. The idea of *forgiving* in the model is also interesting and relatively new. The example presented by the students refers to foods that smell 'bad' for those who are not used to them. Finally, we note that this model is the only one to mention the importance of language in a model of intercultural competence.

Group 5's model seems to be the most interesting one because it combines different ideologies in the objectives it sets and in its use of words. At the centre of the model, which is clearly positioned in the context of MUC, we find the notion of *participation* (illustrated by concrete activities), surrounded on the left by the idea of the *unfamiliar* (e.g. not knowing others' habits), illustrated by drawings of 'cultural' elements from different Minzus (e.g. a Mongolian tent), and to the right by the concepts of *identification and understanding*. Students also included the terms *process* and *ideology*[1] on top of the figure. According to the students, these two terms symbolize the poles of an interculturality continuum, which seem to resemble certain ideologies of critical approaches to intercultural today (e.g. Piller, 2010). MUC's mottos 知行合一 ('Knowledge corresponds with action') and 美美与共 ('Beauty and Beauty', meaning 'beauties co-exist'/'valuing all Minzus to create unity') appear at the top and bottom of the figure.

To conclude this section, we share some reflections on the links between these models and the magic mirror. First, we note that the different groups of students do not necessarily share the same ideologies on interculturality. While some groups appear to be limited to components similar to international models, others are directly influenced by MUC's ideology. Group 5 proposed a model that would seem to take into account the magic mirror approach that we proposed. In fact, this model seems to enable observing the intercultural at a metacognitive level. Unlike the other models, group 5's does not seem to seek to offer turnkey elements or recipes (*respect, go beyond . . .*), but tools to analyse the 'politics' of interculturality (Holliday, 2010).

The fold: what do students recollect from the contributions of the model of Critical and Reflexive Literacy?

This last section is based on the metaphor of the fold to observe what students seem to retain from the course six months later. We contacted the same students through a Chinese social communication network

(WeChat) and asked them to fill in a short questionnaire in English and/ or Chinese on what they seemed to have learned from the course. As a reminder, by the metaphor of the fold, we wanted the students to learn to identify the orientations, ideologies and agendas of different intercultural approaches, and train them to begin to problematize, accept, combine and/or reject them. We examine the 17 students' responses to the following question: 'What do you remember from group work on the intercultural model that you produced?'

The first element observed in the students' responses relates to the concept of culture. Two students mention having developed a simple interest in 'other cultures', especially in relation to other Minzus. They both use the word *nationalities* in English, which is another way of saying *Minzus* in this language:

Excerpt 1 – Student 11

At the end of the course, I pay more attention than ever before in school, in the life and in the different ethnic students' exchanges and contacts; I am also gradually more curious about each Minzu's cultural tradition, and in participating in the activities of some related national culture.

Excerpt 2 – Student 7

The most important influence on me was that I became more interested in different cultures. After the course, I looked up the customs of many different nationalities and cultural habits of different countries, and learned more about the similarities and differences between cultures with an inclusive perspective.

Note that, by introducing the ideologies of differences and similarities and the inclusion of all, Student 7 differs from Student 11, who seems to adopt a more differentialist approach (Dervin, 2016). Student 7's ideologies stem from a critical intercultural perspective (e.g. Abdallah-Pretceille, 2004), which adds to the Minzu ideology that she introduced at the beginning of the excerpt.

The second element that emerges from the students' responses seems to demonstrate that working together in groups has allowed them to explore the theme of *power relations and hierarchies* in intercultural relations. Three students underline this aspect in their responses.

Student 2 returns to the concept of *respect* in his text:

Excerpt 3 – Student 2

I think the thing that has influenced me most is probably that I have learned to understand and respect. The respect which I mentioned is not superficially perfunctory or even slightly contemptuous. It is a serious willingness to understand other cultures, not to put myself in a higher position, but to communicate, and communicate in an equal way.

Here we find a typical culturalist discourse ('serious willingness to understand other cultures', see McSweeney, 2010), but which is modified by a critical and reflexive approach of *modesty* and *questioning of hierarchies*. The student demonstrates that he has understood the potential problems behind the use of the word *respect*, and that he is able to change its potentially superficial characteristics.

Student 4 shares the same thoughts, without any reference to the concept of culture:

Excerpt 4 – Student 4

I realize that many times when we say respect, it's arrogant. We just saw their existence, but we just pretended to be friendly. Maybe we didn't agree with them. After class, I reflected on this. I think when we say respect, it should be a kind of recognition from the heart and believe in our equality. I'm trying to change, too.

She clearly highlights her awareness of a potential performance camouflaged behind the idea of *respecting others*. The notion of equality is invested here to confront *respect* as a problematic tool for labelling and classifying people.

Finally, Student 5 discusses an MUC ideology, which consists in limiting the problem of tolerance to certain Minzus:

Excerpt 5 – Student 5

In school, we often emphasize ethnic tolerance and regional tolerance. However, after learning ethnic education, I realized that the scope of tolerance should not only include ethnic groups and regions. Inclusion should be a concept without boundaries, because we are all human beings. The world is designed to accommodate many people, and it is up to every inhabitant of the earth to complete the process of acceptance. We must understand that human beings are human beings, before there are women and men, and then there are ethnic regions and countries.

The student challenges the hierarchy represented by this ideology and opens it to everyone ('every inhabitant of the earth'; 'human beings'), thus to 'humanize' interculturality. The student seems to show that she was able to unfold one ideology and to fold another universalistic one.

The ideology that seems to have attracted many students is that of stereotyping. Four students refer to it as the element of 'fold work' that most influenced them. For example, Student 2 explains that she understood that her impressions of a politician like Donald Trump, who was highly critical of China at the time, cannot guide her way of speaking about Americans, of imposing the ideologies of the American President on her understanding of the American people she meets.

On the other hand, Student 9 refers to the argument of the possibility to remove stereotypes:

Excerpt 6 – Student 9

In the past, I might have speculated about his or her characteristics because others said that he or she came from a certain place, but now I rarely think so.

This imaginary (*the stereotype is avoidable*, cf. Jussim, 2018), is itself a typical stereotype (an ideology) in some ICE approaches (see Byram, 2020). It's an imaginary because stereotypes never really disappear since they can easily be replaced by another.

Student 15 realizes the 'dangers' of her stereotypes, especially through the education that she has received in China. She claims to have decided to dig into the 'real life of foreigners', instead of relying on knowledge about the 'Other' found in the media or books.

Finally, Student 13 explains that the research work carried out as a team also made her aware of stereotypical and biased descriptions in the media and/or on social media. With her team, they used Western and Chinese online search engines using the keywords of *China*, *Chinese* and *Beijing*. They discovered many and varied positions towards these three keywords. Here is the conclusion drawn by the student:

Excerpt 7 – Student 13

After the course, I will start to learn about their culture by chatting with people from other countries instead of using Chinese websites to search. For example, I will discuss their food culture with some Korean friends.

Again, the approach may seem culturalist ('to learn about their culture'), yet the student shows that, at a methodological level, she wishes to move away from knowledge found in (social) media in order to focus on more 'authentic' information.

Six months after the end of the course, it seems that certain aspects of the proposed Critical and Reflexive Literacy had an (imperfect) influence on the students. Most seem able to unfold certain aspects of interculturality, sometimes superficially (e.g. having developed an interest in other cultures) or more actively (meeting with foreigners to discuss their diversity, rather than relying on what the media say about foreigners).

[Pause]

> You can't change everything you face, but nothing can change until you face it.
>
> (Baldwin, 2017: 15)

This chapter started from the observation that intercultural approaches in education are multifaceted and ideological, and that it is therefore necessary to position oneself clearly in the smörgåsbord of perspectives to deal with interculturality. Based on a very specific context, that of a diverse university in China, we have tried to demonstrate the potential influences of a new approach to interculturality. Working in a Sino-Finnish team, we had to negotiate an approach to teach interculturality to a group of Chinese students. We realized that our opposing ideologies were going to pose problems of understanding and contradictions among our students (Tournebise, 2012). Furthermore, we had realized that the ideologies that are developed in intercultural courses often come from Western worlds and that this represented an unbearable epistemological injustice. Our students, as representatives of Chinese Minzus, are diverse and their rich intercultural experiences must thus be the starting point to reflect on interculturality. Imposing a specific ideology on them would negate these experiences.

The model of Critical and Reflexive Literacy of Intercultural Approaches that we have developed thus refuses to 'format' students by means of a single perspective. Conversely, our approach gave them an opportunity to observe and analyse different intercultural approaches, and perhaps could help them decide for themselves what the intercultural is about and how to prepare to cope with it. Our analyses from the three components of the model (the fold, the handshake and the magic mirror) show that transformations (minimal and contradictory for most students) seem to have taken place. The different activities that were proposed to the students allowed them to ask questions about elements that they had never considered before: translation, (in)compatibility between ideologies, awareness of their own ideologies, the potential danger of using polysemic concepts. This could represent an important first approach to continue to develop their critical and reflexive senses around the notion of interculturality, which is central in their educational context. As we see in our analyses, the students are torn apart between several ideologies: Western hegemonic ideologies (culturalism, but also increasingly postmodern approaches to interculturality); ideologies of the institution where they study; societal and political Chinese ideologies on diversity as well as the ideologies specific to various Minzus. Figure 5.7 illustrates these different elements:

Long-term education and training that would allow students to deepen their knowledge of different approaches but also to become more aware of their own ideologies seems necessary to consolidate and modify the proposed approach.

Our literacy model symbolizes a foundation stone to begin to *face* and *gradually change* ICE (see the quote from Baldwin at the beginning of this conclusion). Without this endeavour, ICE is bound to remain at a superficial level and to miss opportunities to make a difference in a world where interculturality can easily be misused and abused. As university worlds internationalize, we must give the floor to other voices about interculturality, listen to them and provide them with the opportunity to negotiate with us regarding other knowledge about the notion, which has been so far too Euro-/Western-centric (Paraskeva, 2016). Interculturality is often taught, not from the perspective of genuinely diverse paradigms, but mainly on the basis of economic and political ideologies, supported by supranational institutions (Dervin, 2020). We must now continue to identify and transform these ideologies in order to create a space for inclusive educational and research dialogue, which could lead to further discursive multivocality on interculturality.

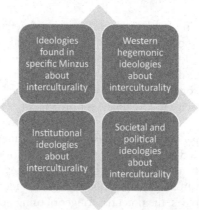

Figure 5.7 Multifaceted ideologies embedded in the students' discourses

[Time to reflect]

- What did you learn about the multifaceted ideologies concerning Minzu in this chapter?
- The students from this chapter all live and study at MUC, a so-called 'Minzu University'. Throughout this book we have presented their voices. Did you get a sense of their study and social experiences at MUC? What seems to be special and – maybe – challenging in this specific context?
- Think about your own educational context, do institutions influence the way people see interculturality by using certain slogans and mottos? Deconstruct them.
- Have you come across 'untranslatables' when you have discussed interculturality with people from other countries? How did you manage to renegotiate their meanings? Have discussions around translating them made these words more 'powerful'?
- The idea of *cultural confidence* is probably unknown to you. What do you make of it? Can you see its potential pros and cons?
- You will be aware of certain models of intercultural competence. What do you know about those who created them? Where are they from? What are their official and 'hidden' affiliations? What do you think influenced them in the way they define intercultural competence? What ideologies seem to emerge from their models?
- Following Jullien (2019), we have tried to help you 'un-build' different approaches to interculturality through considering Minzu. What did you learn about interculturality in the process?

Note

1 Ideology in Chinese is: 思想 (other possible translations: *thought, idea, thinking*). 思 = to think, to consider; ideographic: Weighing something with your mind 田 (field, farm, cultivated) and heart 心. The word in Chinese does not necessarily have a negative connotation and is often linked to politics ('political ideas').

Conclusions

On the importance of companions, complements and alternatives in education

In her work, the philosopher Simone Weil (2005: 259) argues that contradictions are central to life. This is how she puts it: 'The contradictions the mind comes up against – these are the only realities: they are criteria of the real. There is no contradiction in what is imaginary. Contradiction is the test of necessity.' At the end of this book aimed at revitalizing interculturality in education by putting forward a 'Chinese' approach, we argue that, like any other approach to interculturality in education, the complexities and potential contradictions that the notion of Minzu contains in itself and thus adds to world discourses on interculturality are very stimulating. We need contradictions to unveil the complexities of the world. We need contradictions to counter discourses that normalize the exclusion of alternative voices about interculturality and diversity. We need contradictions to resist the constructed 'gaplessness' of ideologies of interculturality that engender one-sided ways of thinking about the notion in research, education and politics. The 'hell' of sameness in ideological constructions of interculturality around the world is contradictory to the very idea of interculturality.

What our book shows is that we cannot be indifferent to alternatives, complements and thus potential companions to the knowledge of interculturality in education. We can agree and/or disagree with these companions. We can identify their similarities and differences. But in order to do so we need dialogue, movement, the *inter-* of the notion of interculturality. The very word *dialogue* in English comes from Greek *dialegein* (διαλέγειν; dia: through/legen: speak) which indicates this movement back and forth between *you* and *us*, and between *us* too.

This book has reviewed how the notion of Minzu is both (co-)constructed and handled by different voices: scholars, experts and Chinese Minzu and international students. In the 'menagerie' of voices that we have presented, different and similar arguments were made by these individuals. At the same time, similarities and differences with other approaches to interculturality were also identified.

The year 2020 might mark a special time for the way we deal with interculturality globally. The many and varied disruptions experienced with the COVID-19 crisis, the new problems that have emerged and the 'old' ones that were acerbated require to revise the ways we have thought about interculturality. From a Chinese perspective, this special context of globalization and the shift of power and attention towards the 'East' that it might trigger means also revising the foci of interculturality. The world has obviously been ignorant of the complexities of China, and there is an urgent need to revise her images and (mis-)perceptions. At the same time, China needs review and modify the ways she has seen the world. As such, like the rest of the world, discourses of interculturality in the Middle Kingdom often rely exclusively on difference. However, as Borges argued (1984: 12): 'We love over-emphasizing our little differences, our hatreds, and that is wrong. If humanity is to be saved, we must focus on our affinities, the points of contact with all other human beings; by all means we must avoid accentuating our differences.' The openings offered by, for example, the One Belt One Road Initiative represent an important counter-voice to a potentially Western-dominated world. Views and epistemologies from the 'West' have 'governed' research and education in the Middle Kingdom and the way interculturality is talked about requires to be modified and added to. What an original perspective such as Chinese Minzu can bring to the world is to unthink and rethink the way we all see diversity from 'within' a nation and 'between' countries. Interculturality is all around in today's China and Minzu as a key notion can allow us to transfer these experiences and the knowledge that derives from them to the rest of the world. There is a need to confront current (dominating) ways of thinking about interculturality with other complex realities. Minzu allows us to consider interactions between diverse people from 'within'.

Our book was based on a bottom-up approach: we started from multiple voices on Minzu issues to deconstruct the notion. What we have learned in terms of attitudes and principles for working on interculturality in education can be summarized by the following four keywords:

- **Attitudes**
  - 真正宽宏大量 (zhenzhengkuanhongdaliang: *genuine generosity*)
    Be open and willing to share and learn about the ways people perceive interculturality.
  - 异境茫然 (Yi jing mang ran; dépaysement: *the feeling of not being at home*)
    Be ready to accept non-understanding about these ways and/or to stand out of your comfort zone by renegotiating meanings of what you have to say and/or what others have to say about interculturality.

- **Principles**

  - 民族知识与认识论 (Minzu zhishilunyurenshilun: *Minzu episte-mology and politics, knowledge and perception of the world*)
    When exploring other ways of 'doing' and reflecting upon intercul-turality it is important to consider the specific epistemological (the way a belief is justified) and political foundations of such perspec-tives. Before judging them, we need to reflect on their pros and cons, differences and similarities with the ones we are comfortable with. We also need to remember that what is constructed as 'unpo-litical' in certain parts of the world, always has to do with politics . . .
  - 反思翻译 (fansifanyi: *Reflexive translation*)
    The use of words is never neutral, thus ideological and poten-tially polysemic. When using several languages to talk about interculturality, we need to reflect systematically (and critically!) on the meanings of the words in and within these languages. For Jullien (2019) it is important to be transparent about one's implicit choices and resources when it comes to language use.

Finally, Figure 6.1 summarizes what we have learned from our work on Minzu as a companion and contribution to interculturality in education.

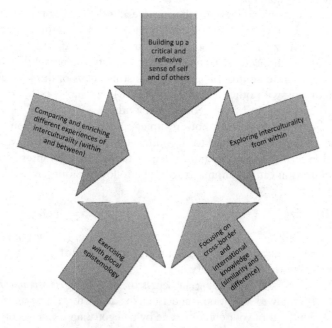

Figure 6.1 Minzu as a companion to interculturality in education

We argue that these represent important components of working on interculturality as a complex notion that can help us unthink and rethink the world we live in. Revitalizing interculturality could take place by taking these components seriously into account.

Before we describe each component, it is important to note:

- The components work hand in hand and should be reciprocal and complementary.
- The components start from what alternative knowledge such as Minzu can bring to discussions of internationalization and interculturality.
- The components are based on the continuum of difference and similarity between people.
- The components emphasize diversity within any given geopolitical space.
- The components suggest comparing and contrasting experiences of interculturality and diversity (e.g. Minzu students and international students in China).

We determine the five components as follows:

1   **Developing a critical and reflexive sense of self and others**. Discourses about any given country are often misleading. For example, 'Western' media often distort certain realities about China, especially when it comes to the internal diversity of China (Minzus). The model thus urges people to adopt a critical and reflexive sense of discussing Chinese affairs with individuals from other countries, and to appreciate and describe critically and reflexively other countries, when compared to China. Reflecting on the pros and cons of comparing countries and contexts and understanding why some people think of certain countries in certain ways are thus necessary. The assumption of the model is that *being able to present, deconstruct* and *reconstruct views about any given country* can lead to more equal and less stereotypical views of 'us' and 'them' and can thus help us meet as equals and avoid creating hierarchies of the 'good', 'bad', 'more civilized', 'less civilized', and so on. This also forces us to be modest about 'us' and 'them'.

   Our model thus requires reflecting critically about the way we present ourselves and others when we meet. This can apply to face-to-face, technology-mediated interaction or (social) media contexts.

2   **Exploring interculturality from within**. This component starts from the assumption that any country can teach us about interculturality *from within* so that we can learn to approach other countries and

contexts in relation to their own internal diversity – while relating it to the 'outside world'. We should also learn to pinpoint the achievements and benefits of diversity and interculturality from within. At the same time, we should strive to improve the ways these are understood, recognized and put into practice in education.

Our model thus requires exploring diversity from within, relating it beyond national borders and, especially, beyond imagined homogeneity.

3   **Focusing on cross-border and international knowledge (similarity and difference).** For the Chinese context, for example, the One Belt One Road (OBOR) era marks a new and important global trend for the world, a space of complex political, economic and intercultural interactions. Minzu can serve as a privileged space to enrich cross-border communication between China and other countries since many Chinese Minzus share linguistic and cultural bonds with other countries. Individuals who study and/or teach in Minzu universities in China can serve as mediators for developing such skills. The assumption of the Model is that through confronting similarities between, for example, Chinese Minzus and cross-border individuals and groups, we could create a strong basis for cooperation with cross-border OBOR.

Our model thus requires rethinking interculturality and internationalization beyond the 'West' and to grab the opportunities offered by alternative knowledge and savoir-faire to propose new perspectives on interculturality within, for example the specific context of cross-border and international interaction. Bearing in mind difference and similarity is an important element of this component.

4   **Glocal epistemology can enrich and contribute to new knowledge about interculturality**. Thinking about internationalization beyond certain accepted but questionable 'Westernized' ideologies (e.g. beyond mere cultural learning, beyond a naive approach to tolerance and democracy) is essential. Minzu relations have been guiding communication between Chinese people for centuries and should inspire others by its rich and varied ways of thinking about and conceptualizing diversity. The assumption of the Model is that by sharing specific conceptions about intercultural dialogue, the world could unthink and rethink internationalization from different perspectives and stimulate alternative dialogues. This could also provide other parts of the world with ideas beyond 'Western' ideologies and stimulate different ways of thinking about intercultural matters.

Our model thus requires looking into different cosmologies about encounters, communication and relations to identify specific and alternative ways of thinking about interculturality and internationalization. Politics and the economy are always integral dimensions of interculturality – wherever we are located on the planet – and must be acknowledged. This entails avoiding criticizing other perspectives for being 'too political' or 'too XXX' (add name of a political party or an ideology) while giving the impression that 'our' approach is politics-free and independent from the economy. If possible, students of interculturality must be introduced to this problematic.

5   **Linking up intercultural phenomena experienced by different kinds of people within and across countries.** As many groups experience forms of mobility, resocialization in potentially different contexts, the use of multilingualism and an interest in diversity, they should be made to cooperate and share their experiences, socialize together and make, for example, internationalization even more international. The assumption of the Model is that when international and local diverse students and staff engage with each other, they can start rethinking the nexus of 'us' and 'them', the meanings of a diverse international campus and develop a more original sense of interculturality. This requires looking into the input of varied groups.

> *Our model thus requires removing the border created by the dichotomy 'insider' and 'outsider' and to compare and contrast experiences of diversity and interculturality within a given context.*

As we can see, the model we propose is not a 'miraculous recipe' for making interculturality happen 'smoothly' or 'effectively' (as many scholars, educators and decision-makers in our neoliberal world would like us to do). Our model urges us to take the time to ponder over what interculturality could be about, how it could happen, what it could entail. It is about enriching this complex *universum* of interculturality – not to simplify it through 'easy steps'. Adding up to the current (limited) cosmology of interculturality is a 'small' step towards revitalizing interculturality in education, by removing the illusion of gaplessness that current research and education present to us.

This book placed the word *companion* at its centre – Minzu as a companion to interculturality in education. The Chinese character for this word, 朋 (peng), which is composed of the repetition of the radical for the moon/month, represents two people walking together. As stated in our introduction, in Ancient Chinese, 朋 meant 'those who shared the same gate'. We hope that with this book we can contribute to opening that 'same gate' and starting new conversations about interculturality.

Bibliography

Abdallah-Pretceille, M. (2004). Interculturalism as a paradigm for thinking about diversity. *Intercultural Education 17*(5), 475–483.

Allport, G. W. (1954). *The Nature of Prejudice*. Boston: Addison-Wesley.

Altbach, P. G. (2004). Higher education crosses borders. *Change 36*(2), 18–24.

Althusser, L. (2001). *Lenin and Philosophy and Other Essays*. New York: NYU Press.

Amsler, S., Kerr, J. & Andreotti, V. (2020). Interculturality in teacher education in times of unprecedented global challenges. *Education and Society 38*(1), 13–37.

Arnaut, K. & Spotti, M. (2015). Superdiversity discourse. In: Tracy, K., Illie, C. & Sandel, T. (Eds.). *The International Encyclopedia of Language and Social Interaction* (pp. 1–7). London: John Wiley & Sons.

Aron, R. (2002). *Dawn of Universal History*. Cambridge, MA: Basic Books.

Aspinall, P. J. & Song, M. (2013). Is race a 'salient . . .' or 'dominant identity' in the early 21st century: The evidence of UK survey data on respondents' sense of who they are. *Social Science Research 42*(2), 547–561.

Atabong, A. (Ed.) (2018). *Antiracism Education in and Out of Schools*. London: Palgrave MacMillan.

Bakhtin, M. (1982). *The Dialogic Imagination: Four Essays*. Dallas: University of Texas Press.

Baldwin, J. (2017). *I Am Not Your Negro*. Paris: Robert Laffont.

Banks, J. (1989). Approaches to multicultural curriculum reform. *Trotter Review 3*(3), 17–19.

Bauman, Z. (2016). Social media are a trap. *Interview with de Querol*. https://english.elpais.com/elpais/2016/01/19/inenglish/1453208692_424660.html

Benjamin, R. (2013). *The Translator Relay: Ross Benjamin*. www.wordswithoutborders.org/dispatches/article/the-translator-relay-ross-benjamin

Benton Lee, M. (2016). Sociological perspectives on ethnic minority teachers in China: A review of the research literature. *Diaspora, Indigenous, and Minority Education 10*(1), 55–68.

Berthoz, A. (2010). *Simplexity: Simplifying Principles for a Complex World*. New Haven, CT: Yale University Press.

Billeter, J.-F. (2006). *Contre François Jullien*. Paris: Allia.

Billeter, J.-F. (2014). *Trois essais sur la traduction*. Paris: Allia.

Birkeland, Å. (2016). Cross cultural comparative education – Fortifying preconceptions or transformation of knowledge? *Policy Futures in Education 14*(1), 77–91.

Blommaert, J. (2015). Commentary: Superdiversity old and new. *Language and Communication: An Interdisciplinary Journal 44*(1), 82–89.

Blommaert, J. & Rampton, B. (2011). Language and superdiversity. *Diversities 13*(2), 1–21.

Borges, J. L. (1984). *Facing the Year 1983: In Twenty-Four Conversations with Borges, Including a Selection of Poems.* Housatonic, MA: Lascaux.

Braun, V. & Clarke, V. (2006). Using thematic analysis in psychology. *Qualitative Research in Psychology 3*(2), 77–101.

Burdsey, D. (2013). The foreignness is still quite visible in this town: Multiculture, marginality and prejudice at the English seaside. *Patterns of Prejudice 47*(2), 95–116.

Byram, M. (2008). *From Foreign Language Education to Education for Intercultural Citizenship.* Clevendon: Multilingual Matters.

Byram, M. (2020). *Teaching and Assessing Intercultural Communicative Competence : Revisited.* Clevendon: Multilingual Matters.

Cassin, B. (2014). Traduire les intraduisibles, un état des lieux. *Cliniques méditerranéennes 2*(90), 25–36.

Chemla, K. & Keller, E. F. (Eds.) (2017). *Cultures without Culturalism: The Making of Scientific Knowledge.* Durham, UK: Duke University Press.

Chen, N. & Dervin, F. (2019). Conclusion: Comparing Chinese and Nordic education systems – Some advice. In Liu, H., Dervin, F. & Du, X. (Eds.). *Nordic-Chinese Intersections within Education* (pp. 293–300). Cham: Palgrave Macmillan.

Cheng, A. (2007). *Can China Think?* Paris: Editions du Seuil.

Clothey, R. & Hu, D. Y. (2014). The impact of a national goal driven higher education policy on an ethnic minority serving institution in China. *Higher Education Policy 28*, 353–368.

Deleuze, G. (1996). *L'Abécédaire de Gilles Deleuze.* Paris: Vidéos Montparnasse.

Dervin, F. (2016). *Interculturality in Education: A Theoretical and Methodological Toolbox.* London: Palgrave.

Dervin, F. (2020). Creating and combining models of Intercultural competence for teacher education/training: On the need to rethink IC frequently. In: Dervin, F., Moloney, R. & Simpson, A. (Eds.). *Intercultural Competence in the Work of Teachers: Confronting Ideologies and Practices* (pp. 57–72). London: Routledge.

Dervin, F., Du, X. & Härkönen, A. (Eds.) (2017). *International Students in China: Education, Student Life and Intercultural Encounters.* London: Palgrave Macmillan.

Dervin, F., Härkönen, A., Yuan, M., Chen, N. & Zhang, W. (2020). "I want to feel that I live in China": Imaginaries and hospitality in international students' (mis-)encounters at a top Chinese university. *Frontiers of Education in China 15*(4), 588–620.

Dervin, F., Moloney, R. & Simpson, A. (Eds.) (2020). *Intercultural Competence in the Work of Teachers: Confronting Ideologies and Practices.* London: Routledge.

Dervin, F. & Simpson, A. (2021). *Interculturality and the Political within Education.* London: Routledge.

de Sousa Santos, B. (2010). A non-occidentalist West?: Learned ignorance and ecology of knowledge. *Theory, Culture and Society 26*(7–8), 103–125.

Ding, X. (2016). Exploring the experiences of international students in China. *Journal of Studies in International Education 20*(4), 319–338.

Dong, J., Du, C., Jeffermans, K., Li, J., Varis, P. & Wang, X. (2012). Chinese in a superdiverse world. In: de Jong, N., Juffermans, K., Keijzer, M. & Rasier, L. (Eds.). *Papers of the Anéla 2012 Applied Linguistics Conference*. Delft: Anéla.

Ellul, J. (1966). *Exégèse des nouveaux lieux communs*. Paris: Calmann-Lévy.

Eriksen, T. H. (2001). Between universalism and relativism: A critique of the UNESCO concepts of culture. In: Cowan, J. K., Dembour, M.-T. & Wilson, R. A. (Eds.). *Culture and Rights: Anthropological Perspectives* (pp. 127–148). Cambridge: Cambridge University Press.

Fang, W. (2019). *Modern Notions of Civilization and Culture in China*. London: Palgrave MacMillan.

Fanshawe, S. & Sriskandrajah, D. (2010). *'You can't Put Me in Box': Superdiversity and the End of Identity Politics in Britain*. London: Institute for Public Policy Research.

Fei, X. (1988). The plural-unity structure of the Chinese nation (Zhonghua Minzu de duoyuan yiti geju). *Journal of Peking University (Beijing Daxue Xuebao) 4*, 1–19.

Ferri, G. (2018). *Intercultural Communication*. London: Palgrave MacMillan.

Fomina, J. 2010. The failure of British multiculturalism: Lessons for Europe. *Polish Sociological Review 4*(156), 409–424.

Freire, P. (1971). *Pedagogy of the Oppressed*. New York: Herder and Herder.

Gao, G. & Ting-Toomey, S. (1998). *Communicating Effectively with the Chinese*. Thousand Oaks, CA: Sage.

Gao, X. & Ren, W. (2018). Controversies of bilingual education in China. *International Journal of Bilingual Education and Bilingualism 22*(3), 267–273.

Garcia, O. & Wei, L. (2014). *Translanguaging, Bilingualism and Education*. New York: Palgrave.

Goffman, E. (1955). On face-work. *Psychiatry 18*(3), 213–231.

Gong, Y. F., Ma, M., Hsiang, T. P. & Wang, C. (2020). Sustaining international students' learning of Chinese in China: Shifting motivations among New Zealand students during study abroad. *Sustainability 12*, 62–89.

Grant, C. A. & Portera, A. (2010). *Intercultural and Multicultural Education: Enhancing Global Interconnectedness*. London: Routledge.

Guo, Z. (2020). *Changing Ethnicity: Contemporary Ethno-Politics in China*. London: Palgrave Macmillan.

Handel, Z. (2019). *Language, Writing and Literary Culture in the Sinographic Cosmopolis* (Vol. 1). Leiden: Brill.

Hansen, V. (2019). *The Year 1000: When Globalization Began*. New York: Scribner.

Harrell, S. (2000). *Field Studies of Ethnic Identity: Yi Communities in Southwest China*. Guilin, CN: Guangxi People's Press.

Hawkins, J. (1978). National-Minority Education in the People's Republic of China. *Comparative Education Review 22*(1), 147–162.

Holliday, A. (2010). *Intercultural Communication and Ideology*. London: Sage.

Huang, B. (2018). Discourses of "Chineseness" and superdiversity. In: Creese, A. & Blackledge, A. (Eds.). *The Routledge Handbook of Language and Superdiversity*. London: Routledge.

Hussain, M. & Hong, S. (2019). A study on academic adaptation of international students in China. *Higher Education Studies 9*(4), 80–91.

Jackson, J. (2018). *Online Intercultural Education and Study*. London: Routledge.

Jiani, M. A. (2016). Why and how international students choose Mainland China as a higher education study abroad destination. *Higher Education 74*, 563–579.

Jin, B. H., Pei, S. Y. and Xiao, R. (2012). Zhonghua minzu: minzu fuheti haishi minzu shiti? [The Chinese nation: 'National complex' or 'national entity'?]. *Heilongjiang Ethnic Series 1*(9), 1–13.

Johansson, M. & Suomela-Salmi, E. (2011). Enonciation: French pragmatic approach(es). In J. Zienkowski, J.-A. Ostman, & J. Verschueren (Eds), *Discursive Pragmatics* (pp. 71–98). Amsterdam: Benjamins.

Jullien, F. (2010). *Les transformations silencieuses*. Paris: Le Livre de Poche.

Jullien, F. (2019). *De l'écart à l'inouï*. Paris: L'Herne.

Jussim, L. (2018). The accuracy of demographic stereotypes. *PsyArXiv*. https://doi.org/10.31234/osf.io/beaq3

Kaufman, J. C. (2009). The sediment of nomadism. *History in Africa 36*, 235–264.

Kell, C. (2013). *Ariadne's Thread: Literacy, Scale and Meaning Making Across Space and Time*. Working Papers in Urban Language & Literacies 118. London: Kings College London.

Kerbrat-Orecchioni, C. (1994). *L'énonciation de la subjectivité dans le langage*. Paris: Armand Colin.

Kim, H. (2010). *International Ethnic Networks and Intra-Ethnic Conflict: Koreans in China*. London: Palgrave.

Lafont, R. (1971). *Le sud et le nord, dialectique de la France*. Toulouse: Privat.

Larbi, F. O. & Fu, W. (2017). Practices and challenges of internationalization of higher education in China; international students' perspective: A case study of Beijing Normal University. *International Journal of Comparative Education and Development 19*(2/3), 78–96.

Leibold, J. (2016). Preferential policies for ethnic minorities in China. In Zang, X. (Ed.). *Handbook on Ethnic Minorities in China* (pp. 165–188). London: Elgar.

Leibold, J. & Chen, Y. B. (Eds.) (2014). *Minority Education in China*. Hong Kong: Hong Kong University Press.

Li, Y. & Dervin, F. (2019). Constructions of social justice, marginalization, and belonging. In G. W. Noblit (Ed.). *Oxford Research Encyclopedias: Education*. Oxford: Oxford University Press.

Liang, S. (2014). Problematizing monolingual identities and competence in Guangzhou in the era of multilingualism and superdiversity. In: Solly, M. & Esch, E. (Eds.). *Language Education and the Challenges of Globalization: Sociolinguistic Issues* (pp. 153–168). Newcastle, UK: Cambridge Scholars Publishing.

Liu, G. (2011). Yi peiyang duoyuan wenhua jiaoshi weimubiao – Xinjiang gaoshi jiaoyulei kecheng shezhi gaige gouxiang [Taking cultivation of multicultural teachers as the goal: The reform of educational curriculum in Xinjiang normal universities]. *Jiaoshi jiaoyu yanjiu 23*(1), 17–22.

Liu, Q., Çolak, F. Z. & Agirdag, O. (2020). Characteristics, issues, and future directions in Chinese multicultural education: A review of selected research 2000–2018. *Asia Pacific Education Review 21*, 279–294.

Liu, Y. & Dervin, F. (2020). Racial marker, transnational capital, and the occidental other: White Americans' experiences of whiteness on the Chinese mainland. *Journal of Ethnic and Migration Studies*.

Longhi, S. (2013). Impact of cultural diversity on wages, evidence from panel data. *Regional Science and Urban Economics 43*(5), 797–807.

Longxi, Z. (1988). The myth of the other: China in the eyes of the West. *Critical Inquiry 15*(1), 108–131.

Lumkes, J. H., Hallett, S. & Vallade, L. (2012). Hearing versus experiencing: The impact of a short-term study abroad experience in China on students perceptions regarding globalization and cultural awareness. *International Journal of Intercultural Relations 36*(1), 151–159.

Ma, R. (2017). Reconstructing "nation" (Minzu) discourses in China. *International Journal of Anthropology and Ethnology 1*(8), 2–15.

Maffesoli, M. (1997). *The Time of the Tribes*. London: Sage.

Makoni, S. (2012). A critique of language, languaging and supervernacular. *Ponta Grossa 1*(2), 189–199.

Mańkowska, A. (2019). Learning and teaching opportunities of ethnic minorities in multicultural China. Unity, diversity or critical pluralism? *Culture – Society – Education 1*(15), 69–81.

Mannheim, K. (1929/2006). *Ideology and Utopia: An Introduction to the Sociology of Knowledge*. Eastford, CT: Martino Fine Books.

Marková, I., Linell, P., Grossen, M. & Salazar Orvig, A. (2012). *Dialogue in Focus Groups*. London: Equinox.

Matusov, E., Marjanovic-Shane, A., Kullenberg, T. & Curtis, K. (2019). Dialogic analysis vs. discourse analysis of dialogic pedagogy: Social science research in the era of positivism and post-truth. *Dialogic Pedagogy: An International Online Journal 7*, 20–62.

McSweeney, B. (2010). A triumph of faith – A failure of analysis Hofstede's model of national cultural difference. *Human Relations 55*(1), 89–118.

Ministry of Education. (2019). *Statistical Report on International Students in China for 2018*. http://en.moe.gov.cn/documents/reports/201904/t20190418_378692.html

Ndhlovu, F. (2015). A decolonial critique of diaspora identity theories and the notion of superdiversity. *Diaspora Studies 9*(1), 28–40.

Nelson, E. S. (2019). *Chinese and Buddhist Philosophy in Early Twentieth-Century German Thought*. London: Bloomsbury.

Neuendorf, K. A. (2017). *The Content Analysis Guidebook*. Thousand Oaks, CA: Sage.

Ou, Q. & Du, N. (2017). Teachers' multicultural awareness and the ethnic identity of minority students: An individual case study of a Hani student. *Frontiers of Education in China 7*, 212–226.

Paraskeva, J. M. (2016). *Curriculum Epistemicide: Towards an Itinerant Curriculum Theory*. New York. Routledge.

Patton, M. Q. (2002). *Qualitative Research & Evaluation Methods*. London: Sage.

Peng, R.-Z., Zhu, C. & Wu, W.-P. (2020). Visualizing the knowledge domain of intercultural competence research: A bibliometric analysis. *International Journal of Intercultural Relations 74*, 58–68.

Pho, H. & Schartner, A. (2019). Social contact patterns of international students and their impact on academic adaptation. *Journal of Multilingual and Multicultural Development*.

Piller, I. (2010). *Intercultural Communication*. Edinburg: EUP.

Postiglione, G. A. (Ed.) (2013). *China's National Minority Education: Culture, Schooling, and Development*. New York: Routledge.

Pu, W. & Liu, Y. (2017). Lun minzu diqu jiaoshi de kuawenhua jiaoyu shiming jiqi hexin suyang [One the intercultural education mission and the core qualities of the teachers in the ethnic regions]. *Guangxi shifan daxue xuebao (zhexue shehui kexueban) 53*, 109–114.

Purchas, S. (2014). *Hakluytus Posthumus or, Purchas His Pilgrimes*. Cambridge: Cambridge University Press.

Qian, M. H. (2010). Ethnic education should undertake the major historic task of ethnic unity and the possibility of and explorations into the localization of diversified education. *Chinese Education & Society 43*(5), 62–76.

Roucek, J. S. (1944). A history of the concept of ideology. *Journal of the History of Ideas 5*(4), 479–488.

Shaules, J. (2019). *Language, Culture, and the Embodied Mind*. Berlin: Springer.

Shi, L, Huang, X.-Q., Shi, L., Tao, Y. F., Yao, Y.-F., Yu, L., Lin, K. Q., Yi, W., Sun, H., Tokunaga, K. & Chu, J.-Y. (2011). HLA polymorphism of the Zhuang population reflects the common HLA characteristics among Zhuang-Dong language-speaking populations. *Journal of Zhejiang University Science B 12*, 428–435.

Simpson, A., Simpson, U., Chen, N. & Dervin, F. (forth). Teaching intercultural communication to English majors in China: Conceptual contradictions and ideological biases?

Song, Y. & Xia, J. (2020). Scale making in intercultural communication: Experiences of international students in Chinese universities. *Language, Culture and Curriculum*.

Spiteri, D. (2017). *Multiculturalism, Higher Education and Intercultural Communication*. London: Palgrave MacMillan.

Spriggs, S. (2018). University life in: China. *Times Higher Education*. www.timeshighereducation.com/student/advice/university-life-china

Strassberg, R. E. (2002). *A Chinese Bestiary: Strange Creatures from the Guideways Through Mountains and Seas*. Berkeley, Los Angeles, London: University of California Press.

Sude, Yuan, M. & Dervin, F. (2020). *Introduction to Ethnic Minority Education in China: Policies and Practices*. Frankfurt: Springer-Verlag.

Swain, M. B. (2011). Myth management in tourism's imaginariums: Tales from Southwest China and beyond. In: Salazar, N. B., Nelson, H. H. & Grabum, H. (Eds.). *Tourism Imaginaries: Anthropological Approaches* (pp. 103–124). New York and Oxford: Berghahn.

Syrett, S. & Lyons, M. (2007). Migration, new arrivals and local economies. *Local Economy 22*(4), 325–334.

Teng, X. (2010). "多元文化整合教育" 与基础教育改革 ["Multicultural integrated education" and curriculum reform of basic education]. 中国教育学刊 [*Journal of the Chinese Society of Education*] *11*, 51–52.

Teng, X. (2012). Cultural diversity and integrated multicultural education. *Frontiers of Education in China 7*(2), 163–168.

Teng, X. & Su, H. (1997). 多元文化社会与多元文化一体化教育 [Multicultural society and multicultural unity education]. 民族教育研究 [*Journal of Research on Education for Ethnic Minorities*] *8*(1), 18–30.

Tian, M. & Lowe, J. A. (2013). Intercultural identity and intercultural experiences of American students in China. *Journal of Studies in International Education 18*(3), 281–297.

Tian, M., Dervin, F. & Lu, G. (Eds.). (2020). *Academic Experiences of International Students in Chinese Higher Education*. London: Routledge.

Tournebise, C. (2012). *Enseigner l'interculturel dans le supérieur: quels discours et approches d'un concept ambigu à l'heure de l'internationalisation?: Le cas de la Finlande*. Turku: Humanoria.

Tsegay, S. M., Zegergish, M. Z. & Ashraf, M. A. (2018). Socio-cultural adjustment experiences of international students in Chinese higher education institutions. *Millenial Asia 9*(2), 183–202.

Turner, B., S. & Khondker, H. H. (2010). *Globalization East and West*. London: Sage.

Varis, P. & Wang, X. (2011). Superdiversity on the internet: A case from China. *Diversities 13*(2), 71–83.

Vertovec, S. (2007). Super-diversity and its implications. *Ethnic and Racial Studies 30*(6), 1024–1054.

Vertovec, S. (2017). Talking around super-diversity. *Ethnic and Racial Studies 42*(1), 125–139.

Wang, W. (2018). Researching education and ethnicity in China: A critical review of the literature between 1990 and 2014. *Frontiers of Education in China 13*(2), 216–244.

Wang, W. & Du, L. (2018). Education of ethnic minorities in China. In: Peters, M. A. (Ed.). *Encyclopedia of Educational Philosophy and Theory*. Singapore: Springer.

Weil, S. (2005). *An Anthology*. London: Penguin Classics.

Wikan, U. (2006). *Generous Betrayal*. Chicago: CUP.

Woodin, J. (2018). *Interculturality, Interaction and Language Learning*. London: Routledge.

Wu, D. Y.-H. (1991). The construction of Chinese and non-Chinese identities. *Daedalus 120*(2), 159–179.

Xing, H. (2001). *Minzu Education Pedagogy*. Beijing: Education Science Press.

Xiong, W. (2020). *Ethnic Minority-Serving Institutions Higher Education Case Studies from the United States and China*. London: Palgrave.

Xiong, W. & Jacob, W. J. (2020). Ethnic minority-serving higher education institutions in the United States and China: A comparative case study of two institutions. *Asia Pacific Education Review 21*, 295–309.

Yang, M. (2017). *Learning to Be Tibetan: The Construction of Ethnic Identity at Minzu University of China*. London: Lexington Books.

Yuan, H. (2018). Educating culturally responsive Han teachers: Case study of a teacher education program in China. *International Journal of Multicultural Education 20*(2), 42–57.

Yuan, M., Sude, Wang, T., Zhang, W., Chen, N., Simpson, A. & Dervin, F. (2020). Chinese Minzu education in higher education: An inspiration for 'Western' diversity education? *British Journal of Educational Studies 68*(4), 461–486.

Yuxin, J., Byram, M., Xuerui, J., Li, S. & Xuerui, J. (2019). *Experiencing Global Intercultural Communication: Preparing for a Community of Shared Future for Mankind and Global Citizenship*. Beijing: Foreign Language Teaching and Research Press.

Zang, X. (Ed.) (2016). *Handbook on Ethnic Minorities in China*. London: Elgar.

Zenz, A. (2014). *Neo-Integrationism, Minority Education and Career Strategies in Qinghai, P.R. China*. Berlin: Brill.

Zhang, D. & Chen, L. (2014). Creating a multicultural curriculum in Han-dominant schools. *Comparative Education 50*(4), 400–416.

Zhang, J. Y. (2015). Minzu diqu jiaoshi de wenhua minganxing jiqi shengcheng [Cultural sensitivity of teachers in ethnic areas and its formation]. *Zhongguo chengren jiaoyu 6*, 80–82.

Zhang, X. (2017). The paradigmatic crises in China's Minzu studies: Reflections from the perspective of human development. *Journal of Chinese humanities 3*(7), 135–155.

Zhao, X. (2014). Zhongguo minzu yanjiu de kunjing jiqi fanshi zhuanhuan [The Dilemmas and Paradigm Shifts in Chinese Nationality Studies]. *Tansuo yu zhengming 4*, 29–35.

Zheng, Y. (2012). Lijiexing wenhua yanjiuzhe: Duoyuan wenhua lijie jiaoyu zhongde jiaoshi juese [Understanding-oriented culture researcher: The role of teachers in education for multicultural understanding]. *Minzu jiaoyu yanjiu 23*(4), 70–74.

Zhou, M. (2012). Historical review of the PRC's minority/indigenous language policy and practice: Nation-state building and identity construction. In: Beckett, G. H. & Postiglione, G. (Eds.). *China's Assimilationist Language Policy: The Impact on Indigenous/Minority Literacy and Social Harmony* (pp. 105–120). New York: Routledge.

Index

Printed in the United States
by Baker & Taylor Publisher Services